contents

2   Flirting with Romance

7   Midsummer Dream

10   Lace Allure

14   Bohemian Frill

17   Dress with Flair

20   Wrapped Attention

22   Pink and So Pretty

25   Hooded Coat

28   Lilac and Lace

31   Dreamy Ruffles

34   Jacket Artistry

38   Winter Enchantments

42   Shawl a-Shimmer

44   Crochet Basics

welcome

When it comes to romantic fashion, crochet shines! Open mesh work, picots, ruffles, a pretty pineapple pattern, and delicate medallions—these details add enchantment at every turn of this stylish collection. Maybe you've got your sights set on a dramatic skirt or lacy shrug. Perhaps you simply want to whip up a trendy accessory. One look at these feminine fashions, and you'll surely fall for all the fabulous designs offered here.

Enjoy!

Romantic Looks Crochet

flirting with *Romance*

Think of lace as a bring-it-on challenge? You'll love this lacy duet.

Designs by Gayle Bunn   Photographs by Tony Lattari

LACE SKIRT
intermediate

SIZES

S (M, L, 1X)
Instructions are written for the smallest size with changes for larger sizes given in parentheses. When only one number is given, it applies to all sizes. *Note:* For ease in working, circle all numbers pertaining to the size you're making.

finished measurements
Hip circumference = 36 (38, 42, 46)"

SHOP
yarn
Grace from Patons
(Art. 246060)
100% cotton; 1¾ oz. (50 g);
136 yds. (125 m); DK weight
• 7 (8, 10, 11) balls #60008 Natural

hook & extras
• Size E/4 (3.5 mm) crochet hook OR SIZE NEEDED TO OBTAIN GAUGE
• ³⁄₈"-wide elastic to fit lower waist measurement
• 1 yard of 54"-wide lining fabric
• Blunt-end yarn needle

PREP
gauge
5½ lps and 12 rows = 4" (10 cm) in Mesh pat. TAKE TIME TO CHECK YOUR GAUGE.

CROCHET
Beg at waist, ch 200 (220, 240, 260) loosely. Taking care not to twist ch, join with sl st to first ch to form ring.
Rnd 1: Ch 3—counts as dc; dc in each ch around; join with sl st to top of ch-3—200 (220, 240, 260) sts.
Rnd 2: Ch 3, dc in each st around; join with sl st to top of ch-3.
Rnd 3: Ch 1, sc in same st as last sl st, ★ch 5, sk next 3 ch, sc in next ch; rep from ★ to last 3 ch, ch 2, dc in first sc—50 (55, 60, 65) lps.
Rnd 4: ★Ch 5, sc in next ch-5 lp; rep from ★ around; end with ch 2, dc in last dc.
Rep last rnd 3 more times for Mesh pat.

Work Band Pattern
Rnd 1: Ch 1, sc in last dc, ★ch 3, sc in next ch-5 lp; rep from ★ around; end with ch 3, sl st in first sc.
Rnd 2: Sl st in first ch-3 sp, ch 2—counts as hdc; 2 hdc in same sp, ★ch 2, 3 hdc in next ch-3 sp; rep from ★ around; end with ch 2; join with sl st to top of ch-2.
Rnd 3: Ch 2—counts as hdc; hdc in each of next 2 hdc, ★ch 2, hdc in each of next 3 hdc; rep from ★ around, ending with ch 2; join with sl st to top of ch-2.
Rnd 4: Rep Rnd 3.
Rnd 5: Sl st in each of next 2 hdc and next ch-2 sp, ch 1, sc in same sp, ★ch 5, sc in next ch-2 sp; rep from ★ around; end with ch 2, dc in first sc—50 (55, 60, 65) lps. Cont in Mesh pat until work from beg measures 7½".
Next rnd (Inc rnd): ★(Ch 5, sc in next ch-5 lp) twice, (ch 5, sc) twice in next ch-5

lp, (ch 5, sc in next ch-5 lp) 7 times; rep from ★ around; end with ch 2, dc in last dc—55 (60, 65, 70) lps.
Cont in Mesh pat until work from beg measures 9½".
Work 5 rnds of Band pat—55 (60, 65, 70) lps. Cont in Mesh pat until work from beg measures 22½".

Sizes S and L Only:
Next rnd (Inc rnd): ★(Ch 5, sc in next ch-5 lp) 9 (8) times, (ch 5, sc) twice in next ch-5 lp; rep from ★ 4 (6) more times, ★★ch 5, sc in next ch-5 lp; rep from ★★ around; end with ch 2, dc in last dc—60 (72) lps.

Size 1X Only:
Next rnd (Inc rnd): ★(Ch 5, sc in next ch-5 lp) 21 times, (ch 5, sc) twice in next ch-5 lp; rep from ★ once more, ★★ch 5, sc in next ch-5 lp; rep from ★★ around; end with ch 2, dc in last dc—72 lps.

All Sizes:
60 (60, 72, 72) lps.
Work 5 rnds of Band pat.
Rnd 1: ★Ch 5, sc in next ch-5 lp, 5 dc in next sc, sc in next ch-5 lp; rep from ★ around; end with ch 5; join with sl st to last dc.
Rnd 2: Sl st in each of next 3 ch of first ch-5 lp, ch 1, sc in same sp, ★ch 5, sc in center dc of next 5 dc, ch 5, sc in next ch-5 lp; rep from ★ around; end with ch 5, join with sl st to first sc.
Rnd 3: Ch 3, 2 dc in same sp, ★sc in next ch-5 lp, ch 5, sc in next ch-5 lp, 5 dc in next

Appropriate for intermediate and experienced crocheters, this glorious skirt has a fairly simple chain-loop motif on top and a more challenging scalloped border along the bottom.

sc; rep from ★ around; end with 2 dc in same sp as first 3 dc; join with sl st to top of ch-3.

Rnd 4: Ch 1, sc in same sp, ★ch 5, sc in next ch-5 lp, ch 5, sc in center dc of next 5 dc; rep from ★ around; end with ch 5; join with sl st to first sc.

Rnd 5: Sl st in each of next 3 ch of first ch-5 lp, ch 1, sc in same sp, ★5 dc in next sc, sc in next ch-5 lp, ch 5, sc in next ch-5 lp; rep from ★ around; end with ch 5; join with sl st to first sc.

Rep Rnds 2–5 once more, then rep Rnd 2 once.

Lower Edging

Rnd 1: Sl st in next ch-5 lp, ch 3, 4 dc in same lp, ★ch 1, 5 dc in next ch-5 lp; rep from ★ around, ending with ch 1; join with sl st to top of ch-3.

Rnd 2: Sl st in each of next 2 dc, ch 1, sc in same sp, ★ch 1, 3 dc in next ch-1 sp, ch 1, sc in center dc of next 5 dc; rep from ★ around; end with ch 1; join with sl st to first sc.

Rnd 3: Ch 3, 2 dc in same sp, ★ch 1, sc in center dc of next 3 dc, ch 1, 3 dc in next sc; rep from ★ around; end with ch 1; join with sl st to top of ch-3.

Rnd 4: Sl st in next dc, ch 1, sc in same sp, ★ch 3, sc in next sc, ch 3, sc in center dc of next 3 dc; rep from ★ around; end with ch 3; join with sl st to first sc.

Rnd 5: Sl st in next ch-3 sp, ch 1, sc in same sp, ★ch 1, 5 dc in next ch-3 sp, ch 1, sc in next ch-3 sp, ch 3, sc in next ch-3 sp; rep from ★ around; end with ch 3; join with sl st to first sc.

Rnd 6: Sl st in next ch-1 and next dc, ch 3—counts as dc; dc in same sp, 2 dc in next dc, 3 dc in next dc, 2 dc in each of next 2 dc, ★sc in next ch-3 sp, 2 dc in each of next 2 dc, 3 dc in next dc, 2 dc in each of next 2 dc; rep from ★ around; end with sc in last ch-3 sp; join with sl st to top of ch-3.

Rnd 7: Sl st in next dc, ch 1, sc in same sp, (ch 3, sk next dc, sc in next dc) 4 times, ★ch 3 sk next dc, sc in next sc, (ch 3, sk next dc, sc in next dc) 5 times; rep from ★ around;

> *"Romance like a ghost escapes touching; it is always where you are not, not where you are. The interview or conversation was prose at the time, but it is poetry in the memory."*
>
> —George William Curtis

end with sc in last sc, ch 3; join with sl st to first sc; fasten off.

FINISHING

Cut lining fabric to measure 40 (42, 45, 48)×34" long. Sew the center back seam, allowing a ½" seam allowance. Hem the lower edge.

Sew the top edge of the lining to the edge of the waistband, stretching the Skirt (if necessary) to fit the lining.

Fold the waistband in half to the WS and sew in position through all thicknesses. Cut elastic to fit the lower waist measurement and insert it through the waistband. Sew the ends together.

RUFFLED SHRUG
experienced ■■ ■■ ■■ ■■ ■■

SIZES
S/M (L/1X)

Instructions are written for the smallest size with changes for larger sizes given in parentheses. When only one number is given, it applies to all sizes. *Note:* For ease in working, circle all numbers pertaining to the size you're making.

finished measurements
Bust = 34/38 (40/44)"

SHOP
yarn
Grace from Patons (Art. 246060)
100% cotton; 1¾ oz. (50 g); 136 yds. (125 m); DK weight
• 9 (11) balls #60901 Tangleo

3 LIGHT

hook & extra
• Size E/4 (3.5 mm) crochet hook OR SIZE NEEDED TO OBTAIN GAUGE
• Blunt-end yarn needle

PREP
gauge
5½ lps and 12 rows = 4" (10 cm) in Mesh pat. TAKE TIME TO CHECK YOUR GAUGE.

CROCHET
PATTERN STITCH
Mesh Pattern (worked over 50 chs)
Foundation row (WS): Sc in 2nd ch from hook, ★ch 5, sk next 3 ch, sc in next ch; rep from ★ to end—12 lps; turn.

Row 1: Ch 5—counts as dc and ch 2; sc in first ch-5 lp; (ch 5, sc in next ch-5 lp) 5 times; 3 dc in next sc, sc in next ch-5 lp; (ch 5, sc in next ch-5 lp) 5 times); ch 2, dc in last sc; turn.

Row 2: Ch 1, sc in first dc; (ch 5, sc in next ch-5 lp) 5 times; 3 dc in next sc, sc in center dc of next 3 dc, 3 dc in next sc, sc in next ch-5 lp; (ch 5, sc in next ch-5 lp) 5 times; join last ch-5 lp with sc in 3rd ch of ch-5; turn.

Row 3: Ch 5, sc in first ch-5 lp; (ch 5, sc in next ch-5 lp) 4 times; ch 5, sc in center dc of next 3 dc, 3 dc in next sc, sc in center dc of next 3 dc; (ch 5, sc in next ch-5 lp) 5 times; ch 2, dc in last sc; turn.

Row 4: Ch 1, sc in first dc, (ch 5, sc in next ch-5 lp) 5 times; ch 5, sc in center dc of next 3 dc, (ch 5, sc in next ch-5 lp) 5 times; ch 5, sc in 3rd ch of ch-5; turn.

Row 5: Ch 5, sc in first ch-5 lp; (ch 5, sc in next ch-5 lp) twice; 3 dc in next sc, sc in next ch-5 lp; (ch 5, sc in next ch-5 lp) 5 times; 3 dc in next sc, sc in next ch-5 lp; (ch 5, sc in next ch-5 lp) twice; ch 2, dc in last sc; turn.

Row 6: Ch 1, sc in first dc, (ch 5, sc in next ch-5 lp) twice; 3 dc in next sc, sc in center dc of next 3 dc, 3 dc in next sc, sc in next ch-5 lp; (ch 5, sc in next ch-5 lp) 4 times, 3 dc in next sc, sc in center dc of next 3 dc, 3 dc in next sc, (sc in next ch-5 lp, ch 5) twice; sc in 3rd ch of ch-5; turn.

Row 7: Ch 5, sc in first ch-5 lp, ch 5, sc in next ch-5 lp, ★ch 5, sc in center dc of next 3 dc, 3 dc in next sc, sc in center dc of next 3 dc,★★ (ch 5, sc in next ch-5 lp) 4 times, rep from ★ to ★★, (ch 5, sc in next ch-5 lp) twice, ch 2, dc in last sc; turn.

Row 8: Ch 1, sc in first dc, (ch 5, sc in next ch-5 lp) twice, ch 5, sc in center dc of next 3 dc, (ch 5, sc in next ch-5 lp) 5 times, ch 5, sc in center dc of next 3 dc, (ch 5, sc in next ch-5 lp) twice, ch 5, sc in 3rd ch of ch-5; turn. Rows 1–8 form Mesh pat.

SHRUG

Note: Shrug is worked in one piece from cuff to cuff with edgings worked after.

Beg at Right Sleeve, ch 42 (50) loosely.
Foundation row (WS): Sc in 2nd ch from hook, ★ch 5, sk next 3 ch, sc in next ch; rep from ★ to end—10 (12) lps; turn.
Row 1: Ch 5—counts as dc and ch 2; sc in first ch-5 lp, (ch 5, sc in next ch-5 lp) 4 (5) times, 3 dc in next sc; sc in next ch-5 lp; (ch 5, sc in next ch-5 lp) 4 (5) times; ch 2, dc in last sc; turn. Row 1 of Mesh pat is now in position.
Inc row (WS): Ch 5—counts as dc and ch-2; sc in first ch-2 sp, work pat across, ending with sc in last ch-5 lp, ch 5, sc in next ch-2 sp, ch 2, dc in 3rd ch of ch-5; turn—½ lp increased at each end of row. Cont in Mesh pat as est, rep Inc row on foll alternate rows 6 more times, then on 4th rows 5 more times—22 (24) lps.
Work 5 rows even in pat, ending with ch 13 for side seam; turn. Remove hook. Using separate length of yarn, join with sl st to opposite end of row and ch 12 for side seam and fasten off. Return hook to ch-13.

Shape Sides

Next row (RS): Sc in 2nd ch from hook, (ch 5, sk next 3 ch, sc in next ch) twice, ch 5, sk next 3 ch; work pat to beg of ch-12 lp; (ch 5, sk next 3 ch, sc in next ch) 3 times—28 (30) lps. Work 3 more rows even in pat.

Shape Right Front

Lp dec row 1 (RS): Sl st in each of first 3 ch, ch 1, sc in same sp; work pat to end; turn.
½ lp dec row 2 (WS): Work pat across, ending with sc in last ch-5 lp; turn. Leave rem sts unworked. Rep last 2 rows 7 (9) more times—20 lps; fasten off.
Next row (RS): Sk first 6 (5) lps; join yarn with sl st in next sc; work pat to end—14 (15) lps.
Work a further 19 rows even in pat for Back, ending with ch 25 (21) for turning ch on last row.

Shape Left Front

Next row (RS): Sc in 2nd ch from hook, (ch 5, sk next 3 ch, sc in next ch) 5 (4) times, ch 5, sk next 3 ch; work pat to end—20 lps. Work ½ lp inc at front edge of next 16 (20) rows—28 (30) lps.
Work 4 rows even in pat; fasten off.

Shape Sides

Next row (RS): Sk first 3 lps. Rejoin yarn with sl st in next sc, pat across 22 (24) lps (Left Sleeve); turn. Leave rem 3 lps unworked. Work 5 rows even in pat.
Work ½ lp dec row on next and foll 4th row 4 more times, then on every alternate row 7 (9) times—10 (12) lps.
Work 1 row even in pat, ending on Row 7 of Mesh pat.

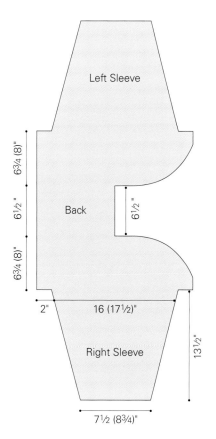

The delicate mesh shrug is worked in one piece from cuff to cuff with the softly ruffled edges added later.

Left Sleeve Edging

Row 1: Ch 1, sc in first dc; (ch 3, sc in next ch-5 lp) 1 (2) time(s); ch 3, sc in center of next 3 dc; (ch 3, sc in next ch-5 lp) 5 times; ch 3, sc in center of next 3 dc; (ch 3, sc in next ch-5 lp) 1 (2) time(s); ch 3, sc in 3rd ch of ch-5; turn.

Row 2: Ch 1, sc in first sc, *3 sc in next ch-3 sp, sc in next sc; rep from * across—41 (49) sc; turn.

Row 3: Ch 1, sc in first sc, *ch 5, sk next 3 sc, sc in next sc; rep from * across; turn.

Row 4: Ch 5—counts as dc and ch 2; sc in first ch-5 lp, *5 dc in next sc, sc in next ch-5 lp, ch 5, sc in next ch-5 lp; rep from * 2 (3) more times, ch 2, dc in last sc; turn.

Row 5: Ch 1, sc in first dc, *ch 5, sc in center dc of next 5 dc, ch 5, sc in next ch-5 lp; rep from * 3 (4) more times, ch 5, sc in center dc of next 5 dc, ch 5, sc in 3rd ch of ch-5; turn.

Row 6: Ch 3—counts as dc; 2 dc in first sc, *sc in next ch-5 lp, ch 5, sc in next ch-5 lp, 5 dc in next sc; rep from * 3 (4) more times, sc in next ch-5 lp, ch 5, sc in next ch-5 lp, 3 dc in last sc; turn.

Row 7: Ch 1, sc in first dc, *ch 5, sc in next ch-5 lp, ch 5, sc in center dc of next 5 dc; rep from * 3 (4) more times, ch 5, sc in next ch-5 lp, ch 5, sc in top of ch-3; turn.

Row 8: Rep Row 4.

Row 9: Rep Row 5.

Row 10: Ch 5—counts as dc and ch 2; *sc in next ch-5 lp, ch 5; rep from * across, ending with ch 2, dc in last sc; turn.

Row 11: Ch 3—counts as dc; 2 dc in first ch-2 sp, *ch 1, 5 dc in next ch-5 lp; rep from * across, ending with ch 1, 2 dc in last ch-2 sp, dc in 3rd ch of ch-5; turn.

Row 12: Ch 1, sc in first dc, *ch 1, 3 dc in next ch-1 sp, ch 1, sc in center dc of next 5 dc; rep from * across, ending with 3 dc in last ch-1 sp, ch 1, sc in top of ch-3; turn.

Row 13: Ch 3—counts as dc; dc in first sc, *ch 1, sc in center dc of next 3 dc, ch 1, 3 dc in next sc; rep from * across, ending with 2 dc in last sc; turn.

Row 14: Ch 1, sc in first dc, *ch 3, sc in next sc, ch 3, sc in center dc of next 3 dc; rep from * across, ending with sc in top of ch-3; turn.

Row 15: Ch 5—counts as dc and ch 2; sc in first ch-3 sp, *ch 3, sc in next ch-3 sp, 5 dc in next ch-3 sp, sc in next ch-3 sp; rep from * 5 (6) more times; ch 3, sc in next ch-3 sp, ch 2, dc in last sc; turn.

Row 16: Ch 3—counts as dc; 3 dc in first sc, *sc in next ch-3 sp, 2 dc in each of next 2 dc, 3 dc in next dc, 2 dc in each of next 2 dc; rep from * 5 (6) more times; sc in next ch-3 sp, 4 dc in 3rd ch of ch-5; turn.

Row 17: Ch 1, sc in first dc, ch 3, sk next dc, sc in next dc, ch 3, sk next dc, sc in next sc; *(ch 3, sk next dc, sc in next dc) 5 times; ch 3, sk next dc, sc in next dc; rep from * 5 (6) more times; (ch 3, sk next dc, sc in next dc) twice; fasten off.

Right Sleeve Edging

With RS facing, join yarn with sl st at corner of Foundation ch; ch 1, sc in corner, *3 sc in next ch-3 sp, sc in rem lp of next sc; rep from * across—41 (49) sc.

Work Rows 3–17 as for Left Sleeve Edging.

Outer Edging/Collar

Sew side and Sleeve seams.

Rnd 1: Join yarn with sl st at right side seam, ch 1 and work 75 (80) sc evenly up Right Front edge to shoulder, 29 sc across Back neck edge, 75 (80) sc down Left Front edge to side seam, and 85 (91) sc across lower Back edge—264 (280) sc. Join with sl st to first sc.

Rnd 2: Ch 1, sc in same sp, *ch 5, sk next 3 sc, sc in next sc; rep from * around, ending with ch 2, dc in first sc.

Rnd 3: 5 dc in next sc, *sc in next ch-5 lp, ch 5, sc in next ch-5 lp, 5 dc in next sc; rep from * around, ending with ch 5, sl st in last dc of Rnd 2.

Rnd 4: Sl st in each of next 3 dc, ch 1, sc in same sp; *ch 5, sc in next ch-5 lp, ch 5, sc in center dc of next 5 dc; rep from * around, ending with ch 5, sl st in first sc.

Rnd 5: Sl st in each of next 3 ch, ch 1, sc in same sp, *5 dc in next sc, sc in next ch-5 lp, ch 5, sc in next ch-5 lp; rep from * around, ending with ch 5, sl st in first sc.

Rnd 6: Rep Rnd 4.

Rnd 7: Rep Rnd 5.

Rnd 8: Rep Rnd 4.

Rnd 9: Sl st in each of next 3 ch, ch 1, sc in same sp, *ch 5, sc in next ch-5 lp; rep from * around, ending with ch 5, sl st in first sc.

Rnd 10: Sl st in next ch-5 lp, ch 3—counts as dc; 4 dc in same lp, *ch 1, 5 dc in next ch-5 lp; rep from * around, ending with ch 1; join with sl st to top of ch-3.

Rnd 11: Sl st in each of next 2 dc, ch 1, sc in same sp, *ch 1, 3 dc in next ch-1 sp, ch 1, sc in center dc of next 5 dc; rep from * around, ending with ch 1; join with sl st to first sc.

Rnd 12: Ch 3—counts as dc; 2 dc in same sp, *ch 1, sc in center dc of next 3 dc, ch 1, 3 dc in next sc; rep from * around, ending with ch 1; join with sl st to top of ch-3.

Rnd 13: Sl st in next dc, ch 1, sc in same sp, *ch 3, sc in next sc, ch 3, sc in center dc of next 3 dc; rep from * around, ending with ch 3; join with sl st to first sc.

Rnd 14: Sl st in next ch-3 sp, ch 1, sc in same sp, *ch 1, 5 dc in next ch-3 sp, ch 1, sc in next ch-3 sp, ch 3, sc in next ch-3 sp; rep from * around, ending with ch 3; join with sl st to first sc.

Rnd 15: Sl st in next ch-1 and next dc, ch 3—counts as dc; dc in same sp, 2 dc in next dc, 3 dc in next dc, 2 dc in each of next 2 dc, *sc in next ch-3 sp, 2 dc in each of next 2 dc, 3 dc in next dc, 2 dc in each of next 2 dc; rep from * around, ending with sc in last ch-3 sp; join with sl st to top of ch-3.

Rnd 16: Sl st in next dc, ch 1, sc in same sp, (ch 3, sk next dc, sc in next dc) 4 times, *ch 3 sk next dc, sc in next sc, (ch 3, sk next dc, sc in next dc) 5 times; rep from * around, ending with sc in last sc, ch 3; join with sl st to first sc; fasten off.

midsummer *Dream*

Yes, this ethereal lace pattern seems fancy, but easy shaping—straight-edge armholes and a rectangular sleeve—makes this cardigan decidedly doable.

Design by Lucille La Flamme
Photograph by Tony Lattari

> "A thing of beauty is a joy forever; its loveliness increases; it will never pass into nothingness."
>
> —John Keats

MESH CARDIGAN
intermediate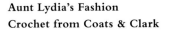

SIZES
S (M, L)
Instructions are written for the smallest size with changes for larger sizes given in parentheses. When only one number is given, it applies to all sizes. *Note:* For ease in working, circle all numbers pertaining to the size you're making.

finished measurements
Bust = 36 (42½, 49)"
Length = 21½ (21½, 22½)"

SHOP
yarn
Aunt Lydia's Fashion Crochet from Coats & Clark (Art. 182); 100% cotton; 150 yds. (137 m); fingering weight
• 8 (9, 10) balls #264 Lime

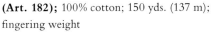

hooks & extra
• Size F/5 (3.75 mm) crochet hook OR SIZE NEEDED TO OBTAIN GAUGE
• Size C/2 (2.75 mm) crochet hook
• Blunt-end yarn needle

PREP
gauge
5 arches and 10 rows = 4" (10 cm) in pat st with larger hook. TAKE TIME TO CHECK YOUR GAUGE.

special stitches
Cluster = Work 2 dc, ch 2, 2 dc in same st.
Picot = Ch 4, sl st back into last st worked.

CROCHET
PATTERN STITCH
(multiple of 11 sts + 1)
Row 1 (RS): Ch 3—counts as dc; 2 dc in first sc, *sk next 2 sc, sc in next sc, ch 5 for arch, sk next 4 sc, sc in next sc, sk next 2 sc, cluster in next sc; rep from * across, ending with 3 dc in last sc; turn.
Row 2: Ch 1, sc in first dc, *ch 5, sc in next arch, ch 5, sc in ch-2 sp of next cluster; rep from * across, ending with sc in top of ch-3; turn.

Row 3: Ch 6—counts as dc and ch-3; sc in first arch, *ch 5, sc in next arch; rep from * across, ending with ch 3, dc in last sc; turn.
Row 4: Ch 1, sc in first dc, *ch 5, sc in next arch; rep from * across, ending with ch 5, sc in 3rd ch of ch-6; turn.
Row 5: Ch 6—counts as dc and ch-3; sc in first arch, *cluster in next sc, sc in next arch, ch 5, sc in next arch; rep from * across, ending with sc in last arch, ch 3, dc in last sc; turn.
Row 6: Ch 1, sc in first dc, *ch 5, sc in ch-2 sp of next cluster, ch 5, sc in next arch; rep from * across, ending with ch 5, sc in 3rd ch of ch-6; turn.
Row 7: Rep Row 3.
Row 8: Rep Row 4.
Row 9: Ch 3, 2 dc in first sc, *sc in next arch, ch 5, sc in next arch, cluster in next sc; rep from * across, ending with ch 5, sc in last arch, 3 dc in last sc; turn.
Rep Rows 2–9 for Pat st.

CARDIGAN
BACK
With larger hook, ch 123 (145, 167).
Foundation row (WS): Sc in 2nd ch from hook, sc in each ch across; turn—122 (144, 166) sc. Work in pat until piece measures 13½" from beg and 33 rows have been worked in pat, ending with Row 9 of pat.

Shape Armholes
Next row (WS): Sl st in each st across to ch-2 sp of first cluster, ch 1, sc in same sp, *ch 5, sc in next arch, ch 5, sc in ch-2 sp of next cluster; rep from * across, ending with sc in ch-2 sp of last cluster; turn. Leave rem sts unworked. Work even in pat until armhole measures 8 (8, 9)"; fasten off.

LEFT FRONT
With larger hook, ch 68 (79, 90). Work Foundation row as for Back—67 (78, 89) sc. Work in pat until 33 rows have been worked in pat, ending with Row 9 of pat.

Shape Armhole
Next row (WS): Ch 1, sc in first dc, *ch 5, sc in next arch, ch 5, sc in ch-2 sp of next cluster; rep from * across, ending with sc in

ch-2 sp of last cluster; turn. Leave rem sts unworked. Work even in pat until armhole measures 8 (8, 9)", ending with Row 9 of pat.

Shape Neck

Row 1 (WS): Sl st across to center of first arch, ch 1, sc in same sp, *ch 5, sc in ch-2 sp of next cluster, ch 5, sc in next arch; rep from * across, ending with ch 5, sc in top of ch-3; turn.

Row 2: Ch 6—counts as dc and ch-3; *sc in next arch, ch 5; rep from * across to last 2 arches, sc in next arch, ch 2, dc in center ch of last arch; turn.

Row 3: Ch 1, sc in first dc, *ch 5, sc in next arch; rep from * across, ending with sc in 3rd ch of ch-6; turn.

Row 4: Ch 6—counts as dc and ch-3; sc in first arch, *cluster in next sc, sc in next arch, ch 5, sc in next arch; rep from * across, ending with ch 2, dc in center ch of last arch; turn. Work even in pat until armhole measures same length as Back; fasten off.

RIGHT FRONT

Work as for Left Front, reversing all shapings.

SLEEVE (make 2)

With smaller hook, ch 57 (57, 62). Work Foundation row as for Back—56 (56, 61) sc.

Rows 1–2: Ch 1, sc in each sc across; turn.
Row 3: Ch 1, sc in first sc, *ch 1, sc in next sc; rep from * across; turn.
Row 4: Ch 1, 1 (1, 2) sc in first sc, sc in each ch-1 sp and sc across; turn—111 (111, 122) sc. Change to larger hook and work in pat until Sleeve measures 21"; fasten off. Place markers on sides of Sleeve 2" down from final row.

FINISHING

Sew shoulder seams.

Edging

Rnd 1: With RS facing and smaller hook, join yarn with sl st in lower corner of Right Front and work one row of sc up Right Front edge, around neck edge, down Left Front edge, and across Back, working 3 sc in corners; join with sl st to first sc.

Rnd 2: Ch 3—counts as dc; work dc, picot, and dc in corner sc; *dc in each of next 5 sc, picot; rep from * around working 3 dc in each corner; join with sl st to top of ch-3; fasten off.

Sew in Sleeves placing sides of Sleeves above markers along unworked sts of armholes to form square armholes. Sew side and Sleeve seams.

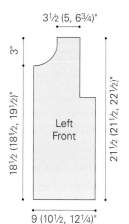

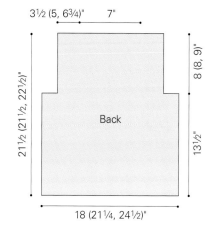

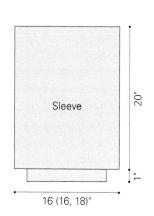

lace *Allure*

Artful handmade accessories express the real you—creative, romantic, and a tad unconventional.

Designs by Svetlana Avrakh   Photographs by Tony Lattari

"If a June night could talk, it would probably boast it invented romance."

—Bern Williams

JULIET CAP
easy ▰▰ ▰▰ ▱ ▱

SIZE
finished measurement
22" in circumference

SHOP
yarn
Brilliant from Patons (Art. 246103)
69% acrylic, 19% nylon, 12% polyester; 1¾ oz. (50 g); 166 yds. (152 m); light worsted weight
• 1 ball #03023 Gold Glow

3 LIGHT

hook & extra
• Size G/6 (4 mm) crochet hook OR SIZE NEEDED TO OBTAIN GAUGE
• Blunt-end yarn needle

PREP
gauge
18 sts and 22 rows = 4" (10 cm) in sc. TAKE TIME TO CHECK YOUR GAUGE.

special stitch
Picot = Ch 2, sl st in last sc made.

CROCHET
Ch 3; join ch with sl st to form ring.
Rnd 1: Ch 3—counts as dc; work 10 dc in ring, join with sl st in 3rd ch of beg ch-3—11 dc.
Rnd 2: Ch 1, sc in same st as joining, ★ch 2, sc in next dc; rep from ★ around, end ch 1; join with hdc in first sc—11 sps.
Rnd 3: Ch 1, sc in top of hdc, ★ch 3, sc in next ch-2 sp; rep from ★ around, end ch 1; join with dc in first sc.
Rnd 4: Ch 1, sc in last dc, ★ch 4, sc in next ch-3 sp; rep from ★ around, end ch 1; join with dc in first sc.
Rnd 5: Ch 1, sc in last dc, ★ch 2, sc in next sc, ch 2, sc in next ch-4 sp; rep from ★ around, end ch 2, sc in next sc, ch 1; join with hdc in first sc—22 sps.
Rnd 6: Rep Rnd 3.
Rnd 7: Ch 1, sc in last hdc, ★ch 3, sc in next ch-3 sp, rep from ★ around, ch 1; join with dc in first sc.
Rnd 8: Ch 1, sc in last dc; ch 2, sl st in last sc—picot made; ★ch 4, sc in next ch-3 sp, make picot; rep from ★ around; end ch 1; join with dc in first sc.
Rnds 9–20: Ch 1, sc in last dc, make picot, ★ch 4, sc in next ch-4 sp, make picot; rep from ★ around; end ch 1; join with dc in first sc.
Rnd 21: Ch 1, sc in first dc, ★ch 3, sc in next ch-4 sp; rep from ★ around; end ch 3; join with sl st in first sc.
Rnd 22: Ch 1, sc in first dc, ★work 2 sc in next ch-3 sp, sc in next sc; rep from ★ around; end work 2 sc in last ch-3 sp; join with sl st in first sc—66 sc.
Rnd 23: Ch 1, sc in each st around; join with sl st in first sc.
Rnd 24: Ch 1, working from left to right, reverse sc in each st around; join with sl st in first st; fasten off. Weave in ends.

Today's trendy take on the Juliet cap is a meshed mix of single crochet and chain stitches.

The scalloped-edge bolero is sensational over a cami.

BRAVA! BOLERO
experienced ■ ■ ■ ■

SIZES
S (M, L, 1X, 2X)
Instructions are written for the smallest size with changes for larger sizes given in parentheses. When only one number is given, it applies to all sizes. *Note:* For ease in working, circle all numbers pertaining to the size you're making.

finished measurements
Bust = 34 (37½, 41, 46½, 53)"
Length = 11½ (12, 13¼, 15, 16)"

SHOP
yarn
Cool Crochet from Bernat (Art. 161074)
70% cotton, 30% nylon;
1¾ oz. (50 g); 200 yds. (182 m); lightweight
• 5 (5, 6, 7, 7) balls #74013 Chocolate

hook & extra
• Size F/5 (3.75 mm) crochet hook OR SIZE NEEDED TO OBTAIN GAUGE
• Blunt-end yarn needle

PREP
gauge
6 arches and 13 rows = 4" (10 cm) over pat.
TAKE TIME TO CHECK YOUR GAUGE.

special stitch
Picot = Ch 3, sl st in top of last sc worked.

CROCHET
PATTERN STITCH
Arch Pattern
(multiple of 4 sts + 2)
Foundation row (RS): Sc in 2nd ch from hook, ★ch 4, sk next 3 ch, sc in next ch; rep from ★ across; turn.
Row 1: Ch 6—counts as tr and ch-2; sc in first ch-4 sp, make picot, ★ch 4, sc in next ch-4 sp, make picot; rep from ★ to last sc, ch 2, tr in last sc; turn.
Row 2: Ch 1, sc in first tr, sk next ch-2 sp and sc, ★ch 4, sc in next ch-4 sp, make picot;

rep from ★ to last ch-6 sp, ch 4, sc in 4th ch of ch-6; turn. Rep Rows 1–2 for Arch pat.

BOLERO
BACK
Ch 106 (114, 126, 142, 162).
Work Foundation row and Rows 1–2 of Arch pat—26 (28, 31, 35, 40) arches.
Work 10 (12, 14, 16, 18) rows more in pat; fasten off.

Shape Armholes
Row 1: Sk first 1 (2, 3, 5, 6) ch-4 sp(s); join yarn with sl st to next ch-4 sp, ch 1, sc in same sp, work in pat to last 2 (3, 4, 6, 7) ch-4 sps, sc in next ch-4 sp; turn. Leave rem sts unworked.
Row 2: Sl st in first ch-4 sp, ch 1, sc in same sp, work in pat to last ch-4 sp, sc in last ch-4 sp; turn. Leave rem sts unworked.
Rep last row 3 more times—19 (19, 20, 20, 23) arches. Work 18 (18, 18, 22, 24) rows even in pat; fasten off.

LEFT FRONT
Ch 26 (30, 34, 38, 42).
Foundation row (RS): Sc in 2nd ch from hook, ★ch 4, sk next 3 ch, sc in next ch; rep from ★ across; turn—6 (7, 8, 9, 10) arches.
Row 1: Ch 7—counts as tr and ch-3; sc in first ch-4 sp, make picot, ch 4, sc in same ch-4 sp, make picot, work in pat to last sc, ch 2, tr in last sc; turn.
Row 2: Ch 1, sc in first tr, sk next ch-2 sp and sc, work in pat to last ch-7 sp, ch 4, sc in 3rd ch of last ch-7; turn.
Rep Rows 1–2 for 5 (6, 7, 8, 9) more times—12 (14, 16, 18, 20) arches.

Shape Armhole
Row 1: Ch 6—counts as tr and ch-2; sc in first ch-4 sp, make picot, work in pat to last 2 (3, 4, 6, 7) ch-4 sps, sc in next ch-4 sp; turn. Leave rem sts unworked.
Row 2: Sl st in first ch-4 sp, ch 1, sc in same sp, work in pat to last ch-6 sp, ch 4, sc in 4th ch of ch 6; turn.
Row 3: Ch 6—counts as tr and ch-2; sc in first ch-4 sp, make picot, work in pat to last ch-4 sp, sc in last ch-4 sp; turn.
Leave rem sts unworked.

Rows 4–5: Work as for Rows 2–3.

Row 6: Ch 6, sc in first ch-4 sp, make picot, work in pat to last ch-6 sp, ch 4, sc in 4th ch of ch 6; turn—7 (8, 9, 9, 10) arches.

Shape Neck

Row 1: Sl st in first ch-4 sp, ch 1, sc in same sp, work in pat to last ch-6 sp, ch 4, sc in 4th ch of ch 6; turn.

Row 2: Ch 6, sc in first ch-4 sp, make picot, work in pat to last ch-4 sp, sc in last ch-4 sp; turn.

Leave rem sts unworked.

Row 3: Ch 6—counts as tr and ch-2; sc in first ch-4 sp, make picot, work in pat to last sc, ch 2, tr in last sc; turn.

Row 4: Ch 1, sc in first tr, sk next ch-2 sp and sc, work in pat to last ch-6 sp, ch 4, sc in 4th ch of ch 6; turn.

Rep Rows 1–4 for 1 (2, 2, 2, 3) more time(s), then rep Rows 1–2 once—4 (4, 5, 5, 5) arches.

Work even in pat until Front measures same length as Back; fasten off.

RIGHT FRONT

Work as for Left Front, noting RS of work becomes WS of work to reverse shaping.

SLEEVE (make 2)

Ch 66 (66, 66, 70, 74).

Work Foundation row and Rows 1–2 of Arch pat—16 (16, 16, 17, 18) arches.

Work 12 rows more in pat.

Shape Sleeve Sides

Row 1 (RS): Ch 8—counts as tr and ch-4; sc in first ch-4 sp, make picot, work in pat to last sc, ch 4, tr in last sc; turn.

Row 2: Ch 6—counts as tr and ch-2; in first ch-4 sp work sc, make picot, ch 4, sc, and make picot; work in pat to last ch-8 sp, ch 4; in last ch-8 sp, work sc, make picot, ch 4, sc, and make picot; ch 2, tr in 4th ch of same ch-8; turn.

Row 3: Ch 1, sc in first tr, ch 4, sk next ch-2 sp and sc, work in pat to last ch-6 sp, ch 4, sc in 4th ch of ch-6; turn—19 (19, 19, 20, 21) arches.

Row 4: Ch 6—counts as tr and ch-2; work in pat to last ch-4 sp and sc, sc in last ch-4 sp, ch 2, tr in last sc; turn. Rep Rows 3–4 until Sleeve measures 7", ending with RS facing for next row; fasten off.

Shape Top of Sleeve

Row 1: Sk first ch-4 sp; join yarn with sl st to next ch-4 sp, sc in same sp, work in pat to last 2 ch-4 sps, sc in next ch-4 sp; turn. Leave rem sts unworked. Work 8 (8, 10, 12, 14) rows even in pat.

Next row: Sl st in first ch-4 sp, ch 1, sc in same sp, work in pat to last 2 ch-4 sps, sc in

next ch-4 sp; turn. Leave rem sts unworked. Rep last row until there are 4 (4, 4, 5, 6) arches; fasten off.

FINISHING

Sew shoulder seams. Sew Sleeve seams. Sew in Sleeves. Weave in ends.

Body Edging

Rnd 1: With RS facing, join yarn with sl st at left shoulder seam, ch 1 and work 1 row of sc evenly around outer edge (the row of sc must be a multiple of 8 sts); join with sl st to first sc.

Rnd 2: Ch 1, sc in same sp as last sl st, ★sk next 3 sc, 8 tr in next sc, sk next 3 sc, sc in next sc; rep from ★ around, omitting sc at end of last rep; join with sl st to first sc; fasten off.

Sleeve Edging

Rnd 1: With RS facing, join yarn with sl st at Sleeve seam, ch 1 and work 64 (64, 64, 72, 72) sc evenly around; join with sl st to first sc.

Rnd 2: Work as Rnd 2 of body edging.

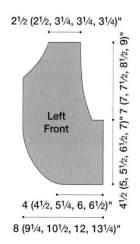

2½ (2½, 3¼, 3¼, 3¼)"

4½ (5, 5½, 6½, 7)" 7 (7, 7½, 8½, 9)"

4½ (5, 5½, 6½, 7)"

Left Front

4 (4½, 5¼, 6, 6½)"

8 (9¼, 10½, 12, 13¼)"

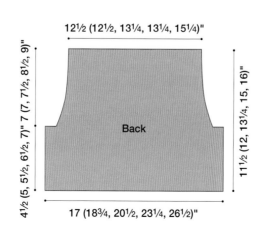

12½ (12½, 13¼, 13¼, 15¼)"

11½ (12, 13¼, 15, 16)"

Back

17 (18¾, 20½, 23¼, 26½)"

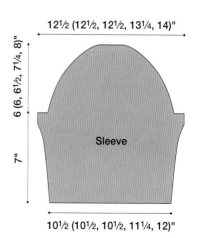

12½ (12½, 12½, 13¼, 14)"

6 (6, 6½, 7¼, 8)"

7"

Sleeve

10½ (10½, 10½, 11¼, 12)"

bohemian Frill

Pineapple lace, typically used for doilies, is ripe for a fashion transformation. As an inset on the front of this cotton shirt, it's fabulously feminine.

Design by Kathryn Merrick   Photograph by Tony Lattari

SHIRT INSET
intermediate

SIZE
One size fits most.

finished measurements
10½×15"

SHOP
yarn
Creative Focus Cotton from Nashua Handknits

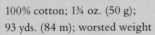

100% cotton; 1¾ oz. (50 g); 93 yds. (84 m); worsted weight
• 3 balls #018 Caribbean

hook & extras
• Size F/5 (3.75 mm) crochet hook OR SIZE NEEDED TO OBTAIN GAUGE
• Sewing thread to match yarn
• Sewing needle
• Blunt-end yarn needle

PREP
gauge
18 sc = 4" (10 cm). First 12 rows of edging measure 4" (10 cm) high. TAKE TIME TO CHECK YOUR GAUGE.

stitch abbreviations
Dc2tog = (Yo and draw up a lp in specified st, yo and draw through 2 lps on hook) twice; yo and draw through all lps on hook.
V-st = (Dc, ch 1, dc) in same st.

special stitches
Arch = *(Yo and draw up a lp, yo and draw through 2 lps on hook)** in st just worked, sk next 2 sts; rep from * to ** in next st, yo and draw through all lps on hook.
Cluster = (Yo and draw up a lp, yo and draw through 2 lps on hook) 3 times in specified st, yo and draw through all lps on hook.
Shell = (2 dc, ch 1, 2 dc) in same st.

CROCHET
Beg at base, ch 47.
Row 1 (WS): Sc in 2nd ch from hook, sc in each ch across; turn—46 sts.
Row 2: Ch 4—counts as hdc and ch 2; sk first sc, *sk next 2 sc, hdc in next sc, ch 2; rep from *, ending with hdc in last sc—15 ch-2 sps; turn.
Row 3: Ch 1, *sc in next hdc, 2 sc in next ch-2 sp; rep from *, ending last rep with sc in 4th and 3rd ch of turning ch, sc in 2nd ch of turning ch—46 sc; turn.
Rows 4–5: Rep Rows 2–3.
Row 6: Ch 3—counts as dc; sk first sc, V-st in next sc, *sk next 2 sc, V-st in next sc; rep from * across, ending with sk next sc, dc in last sc—15 V-sts; turn.
Row 7: Ch 1, sc in each dc and ch-1 sp across; do not sc in top of ch-3—46 sc; turn.
Rows 8–9: Rep Rows 6–7.
Rows 10–11: Rep Rows 2–3.
Row 12: Rep Row 2.
Row 13: Rep Row 3, inc 1 sc in center of row—47 sts.
Row 14: Ch 3—counts as dc; sk first sc, work (dc, ch 1) twice in next sc, arch, *(ch 1,

dc, ch 1) in st just worked, arch; rep from ★ across, ending with dc in st just worked (last st); turn.

Row 15: Ch 1, sc in each dc and ch-1 sp across; do not sc in arch sts—47 sc; turn.

Rows 16–17: Rep Rows 14–15, work 1 st less in center of Row 15—46 sc.

Row 18: Rep Row 2.

Row 19: Ch 5—counts as dc and ch 2; sk first 3 sc, ★cluster in next sc, ch 2, sk next 2 sc; rep from ★ across, ending with dc in last sc; turn.

Right Half

(Work each half separately.)

Row 20 (RS): Ch 1, sc in first dc; (2 sc in next ch-2 sp, sc in next cluster) 7 times; sc in next ch-2 sp; turn, leaving rem sts unworked—23 sc.

Row 21: Ch 1, sc in each of next 3 sc, 2 sc in next sc, ch 3, sk next 3 sc, sc in next sc, sk next 4 sc, 9 dc in next sc, sk next 4 sc, sc in next sc, ch 3, sk next 3 sc, sc in each of last 2 sc; turn.

Row 22: Ch 3—counts as dc; sk first sc, 2 dc in next sc, (ch 1, dc) in each of next 9 dc, ch 1, sk next sc and ch-3 sp, 3 dc in next sc, dc in each sc to end; turn.

Row 23: Ch 3, sk first dc, dc in each of next 3 dc, 3 dc in next dc, ch 3, sk next 2 dc and ch-1 sp and dc; (sc in next ch-1 sp, ch 3) 8 times; end with sk next 2 dc, 3 dc in last dc; turn.

Row 24: Ch 3, 2 dc in first dc, sk first ch-3 sp, (ch 3, sc in next ch-3 sp) 7 times; ch 3, sk next ch-3 sp and 2 dc, 3 dc in next dc, dc in each dc to end; turn.

Row 25: Ch 3, sk first dc, dc2tog over next 2 dc, dc in next dc, 3 dc in next dc, sk next ch-3 sp; (ch 3, sc in next ch-3 sp) 6 times; ch 3, sk next ch-3 sp and 2 dc, 2 dc in last dc; turn.

Row 26: Ch 3, V-st in first dc, sk first ch-3 sp; (ch 3, sc in next ch-3 sp) 5 times; ch 3, sk next ch-3 sp and 2 dc, shell in next dc, dc in each of last 3 dc; turn.

Row 27: Ch 3, sk first dc, dc in each of next 2 dc, shell in ch-1 sp of next shell, sk next ch-3 sp; (ch 3, sc in next ch-3 sp) 4 times; ch 3, shell in ch-1 sp of next V-st, dc in last dc; turn.

Row 28: Ch 3, 2 dc in first dc, shell in ch-1 sp of next shell, sk next ch-3 sp; (ch 3, sc in next ch-3 sp) 3 times; ch 3, shell in ch-1 sp of next shell, 3 dc in next dc, dc in each of next 2 dc; turn.

Row 29: Ch 3, sk first dc, dc in next dc, 3 dc in next dc, ch 2, shell in ch-1 sp of next shell, sk next ch-3 sp, (ch 3, sc in next ch-3 sp) twice; ch 3, shell in ch-1 sp of next shell, ch 2, sk next 2 dc, 3 dc in last dc; turn.

Row 30: Ch 3, in first dc work dc, ch 1, and 2 dc; ch 2, shell in ch-1 sp of next shell, ch 3, sk next ch-3 sp, sc in next ch-3 sp, ch 3, shell in ch-1 sp of next shell, ch 2, sk next 2 dc, shell in next dc, dc in each of last 2 dc; turn.

Row 31: Ch 1, sc in each of first 4 sts, sc in next ch-1 sp, ch 3, sc in ch-1 sp of next shell, 9 dc in next sc, sc in ch-1 sp of next shell, ch 3, sc in each of last 2 sts; turn.

Rows 32–41: Rep Rows 22–31.

Row 42: Ch 1, sc in each of first 2 sc, 3 dc in next ch-3 sp, sc in each of next 9 dc, 3 dc in next ch-3 sp, sc in each sc to end; fasten off.

Left Half

With RS facing, join yarn with sc in center ch-2 sp of Row 19; (sc in next cluster, 2 sc in next ch-2 sp) 7 times; sc in last dc—23 sc; turn. Work as for Right Half.

FINISHING

Edging

With RS facing, join yarn with sl st at top right corner of Inset, work evenly in sc along right side, lower edge, and left side; fasten off.

Neck Edging and Ties

Join yarn with sl st at top inner corner of Left Half, work 14 sc evenly down neck edge, ch 90, sl st in 2nd ch from hook and in each ch back to neck edge—tie made; work evenly in sc along remainder of left neck edge and up right front neck edge to corresponding point of first tie; work a 2nd tie as before, then work 14 more sc evenly to top of right neck; fasten off. Block to proportions.

On a flat surface, pin the Inset to the garment. With a needle and thread, sew the Inset to the shoulders of the garment and around the outside edging. Trim fabric from the garment on the inside, leaving a ¾" seam allowance. Press the seam allowance to the WS; sew in place.

"*A tramp, a gentleman, a poet, a dreamer, a lonely fellow, always hopeful of romance and adventure.*"

—Charlie Chaplin

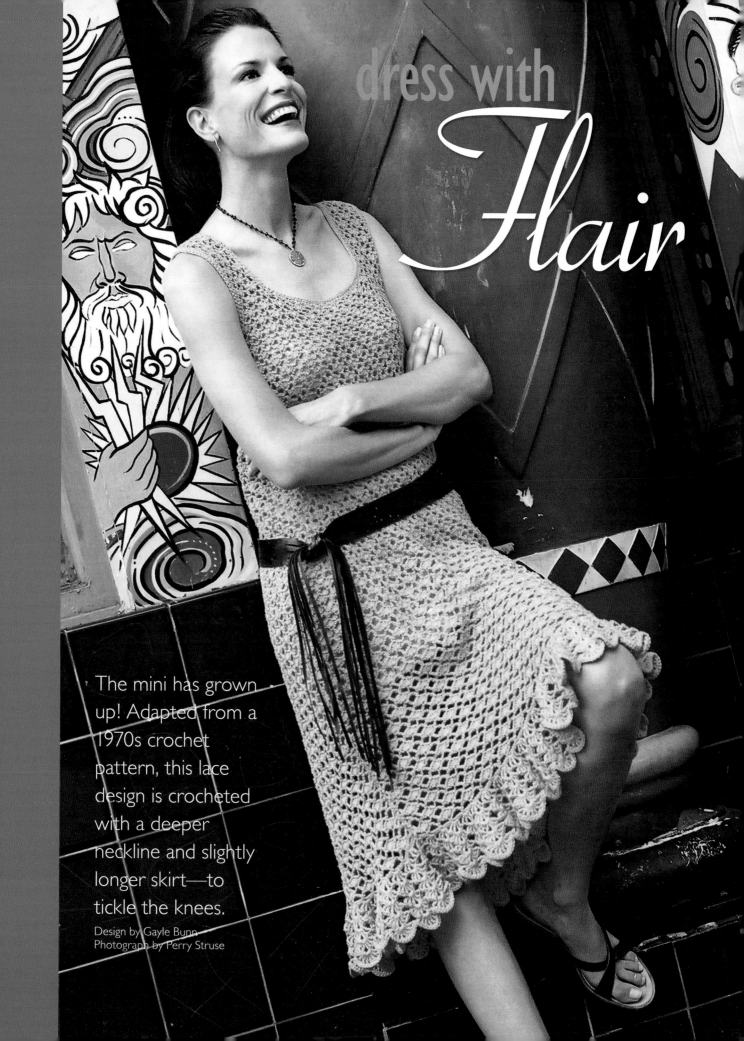

dress with *Flair*

The mini has grown up! Adapted from a 1970s crochet pattern, this lace design is crocheted with a deeper neckline and slightly longer skirt—to tickle the knees.

Design by Gayle Bunn
Photograph by Perry Struse

MINI DRESS
intermediate ■ ■ ■ □

SIZES

M (L)

Instructions are written for the smallest size with changes for the larger size given in parentheses. When only one number is given, it applies to both sizes. *Note:* For ease in working, circle all numbers pertaining to the size you're making.

finished measurements
Bust = 37 (41)"
Length = 37 (37½)"

SHOP

yarn
**Grace from Patons
(Art. 246060)**
100% cotton; 1¾ oz. (50 g);
136 yds. (125 m); DK weight
• 15 (17) balls #60604 Terracotta

hook & extra
• Size D/3 (3.25 mm) crochet hook OR
  SIZE NEEDED TO OBTAIN GAUGE
• Blunt-end yarn needle

PREP

gauge
Skirt: 5½ lps and 12 rows = 4" (10 cm) in
Ch-5 Lp pat.
Bodice: 7 lps and 15 rows = 4" (10 cm) in
Ch-3 Lp pat. TAKE TIME TO CHECK
YOUR GAUGE.

CROCHET

BACK
★★Beg at lower edge, ch 138 (154) loosely.
Row 1 (WS): Sc in 2nd ch from hook; ★ch 5, sk next 3 ch, sc in next ch; rep from ★ across—34 (38) lps; turn.
Row 2: Ch 5—counts as dc and ch-2; ★sc in next ch-5 lp, 5 dc in next sc, sc in next ch-5 lp, ch 5; rep from ★ across, ending with ch 2, dc in last sc; turn.
Row 3: Ch 1, sc in first dc; ★ch 5, sc in center dc of next 5-dc-group, ch 5, sc in next ch-5 lp; rep from ★ across, ending with ch 5, sc in 3rd ch of turning ch; turn.

Row 4: Ch 5—counts as dc and ch-2; sc in next ch-5 lp; ★ch 5, sc in next ch-5 lp, 5 dc in next sc, sc in next ch-5 lp; rep from ★ across, ending with ch 2, dc in last sc; turn.
Row 5: Ch 1, sc in first dc; ★ch 5, sc in next ch-5 lp, ch 5, sc in center dc of next 5-dc-group; rep from ★ across, ending with ch 5, sc in 3rd ch of turning ch; turn.
Rep Rows 2–5 until Back measures approx 12" from beg, ending with Row 4 of pat. The following rows cont in same fashion but with ch-4 lps instead of ch-5 lps.
Row 1 (WS): Ch 1, sc in first dc; ★ch 4, sc in next ch-5 lp, ch 4, sc in center dc of next 5-dc-group; rep from ★ across, ending with ch 4, sc in 3rd ch of turning ch; turn.
Row 2: Ch 5—counts as dc and ch-2; ★sc in next ch-4 lp, 4 dc in next sc, sc in next ch-4 lp, ch 4; rep from ★ across, ending with ch 2, dc in last sc; turn.
Row 3: Ch 1, sc in first dc; ★ch 4, sc in sp bet 2nd and 3rd dc of next 4-dc-group, ch 4, sc in next ch-4 lp; rep from ★ across, ending with ch 4, sc in 3rd ch of turning ch; turn.
Row 4: Ch 5—counts as dc and ch-2; sc in next ch-4 lp; ★ch 4, sc in next ch-4 lp, 4 dc in next sc, sc in next ch-4 lp; rep from ★ across, ending with ch 2, dc in last sc; turn.
Row 5: Ch 1, sc in first dc; ★ch 4, sc in next ch-4 lp, ch 4, sc in sp bet 2nd and 3rd dc of next 4-dc-group; rep from ★ across, ending with ch 4, sc in 3rd ch of turning ch; turn.
Rep Rows 2–5 for Ch-4 Lp pat until Back measures approx 21½" from beg, ending with Row 4 of pat. The foll rows cont in same fashion but with ch-3 lps instead of ch-4 lps.
Row 1 (WS): Ch 1, sc in first dc; ★ch 3, sc in next ch-4 lp, ch 3, sc in sp bet 2nd and 3rd dc of next 4-dc-group; rep from ★ across, ending with ch 3, sc in 3rd ch of turning ch; turn.
Row 2: Ch 3—counts as hdc and ch 1; ★sc in next ch-3 lp, 3 dc in next sc, sc in next ch-3 lp, ch 3; rep from ★ across; end with ch 1, hdc in last sc; turn.
Row 3: Ch 1, sc in first hdc; ★ch 3, sc in center dc of next 3-dc-group, ch 3, sc in next ch-3 lp; rep from ★ across; end with ch 3, sc in 2nd ch of turning ch; turn.

Row 4: Ch 3—counts as hdc and ch 1; sc in next ch-3 lp; *ch 3, sc in next ch-3 lp, 3 dc in next sc, sc in next ch-3 lp; rep from * across, ending with ch 1, hdc in last sc; turn.

Row 5: Ch 1, sc in first hdc; *ch 3, sc in ch-3 lp, ch 3, sc in center dc of next 3-dc-group; rep from * across, ending with ch 3, sc in 2nd ch of turning ch; turn.

Shape Armhole

Row 1: Sl st in first sc and each of next (3 ch and sc) 4 times, sl st in each of next 2 ch, 3 dc in next sc.
*Sc in next ch-3 lp, ch 3, sc in next ch-3 lp, 3 dc in next sc; rep from * across to last 5 lps, sl st in next ch-3 lp; turn, leaving rem sts unworked.

Row 2: Sl st in each of first 2 dc; *ch 3, sc in next ch-3 lp, ch 3, sc in center dc of next 3-dc-group; rep from * across, ending with sl st in center dc of last 3-dc-group; turn.

Row 3: Sl st in each of first 2 ch, 3 dc in next sc; *sc in next ch-3 lp, ch 3, sc in next ch-3 lp, 3 dc in next sc; rep from * across, ending with sl st in last ch-3 lp; turn.

Row 4: Sl st in each of first 2 dc, ch 1, sc in same sp; *ch 3, sc in next ch-3 lp, ch 3, sc in center dc of next 3-dc-group; rep from * across, ending with sc in center dc of last 3-dc-group; turn—22 (26) lps.**
Work even in pat for 10 more rows.

Shape Back Neck

Next row (RS): Ch 3—counts as hdc and ch 1; sc in next ch-3 lp. (Ch 3, sc in next ch-3 lp, 3 dc in next sc, sc in next ch-3 lp) 1 (2) time(s), ch 3, sc in next ch-3 lp, ch 1, hdc in next sc; turn.
Leave rem sts unworked.
Work even in pat on rem 4 (6) lps until armhole measures approx 7 (7½)". Fasten off.
With RS facing, sk next 14 lps; join yarn with sl st to next sc; ch 3—counts as hdc and ch 1; sc in next ch-3 lp, (ch 3, sc in next ch-3 lp, 3 dc in next sc, sc in next ch-3 lp) 1 (2) time(s), ch 3, sc in next ch-3 lp, ch 1, hdc in last sc; turn.
Work even in pat on rem 4 (6) lps until armhole measures approx 7 (7½)".
Fasten off.

FRONT

Work from ** to ** as for Back.
Work even in pat for 2 more rows.

Shape Neck

Work as for Back.

FINISHING

Sew shoulder and side seams.

Lower Edging

Rnd 1: With RS facing, join yarn with sl st at either side seam on bottom edge, ch 1; work 4 sc in each ch-3 lp around; join with sl st to first sc.

Rnd 2: Ch 5—counts as tr and ch 1; tr in same sp as last sl st. *Sk next 3 sc, in next sc work (tr, ch 1) 3 times; tr in same st; rep from * to last 4 sc, sk next 3 sc, in next sc work (tr, ch 1) twice, sl st in 4th ch of beg ch.

Rnds 3–4: Ch 5—counts as tr and ch 1; in same ch work (tr, ch 1, tr); in center ch-1 sp of each tr-group around work (tr, ch 1) 5 times; tr in same sp; work to last tr-group; in last group work (tr, ch 1) 3 times in 2nd ch-1 sp; sl st in 4th ch of beg ch.

Rnds 5–6: Ch 5—counts as tr and ch 1; in first ch-1 sp work (tr, ch 1) twice, tr in same sp; in center ch-1 sp of each tr-group around work (tr, ch 1) 7 times, tr in same sp; work to last tr-group; in last group work (tr, ch 1) 4 times in center ch-1 sp; sl st in 4th ch of beg ch.

Rnd 7: Ch 1, sc in each tr and ch-1 sp around; join with sl st to first sc. Fasten off.

Armhole Edging

With RS facing, join yarn with sl st at side seam. Work 2 rnds of sc evenly around armhole edge, joining each rnd with sl st in first sc. Fasten off.

Neck Edging

With RS facing, join yarn with sl st at shoulder seam. Work 2 rnds of sc evenly around neck edge, working sc2tog in corners and joining each rnd with sl st in first sc. Fasten off.

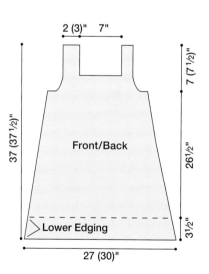

2 (3)" 7"

7 (7½)"

37 (37½)"

Front/Back

26½"

3½"

▷ Lower Edging

27 (30)"

wrapped Attention

Rows of half double crochet and a decorative border form this basic shawl triangle. Make it in a sablelike yarn and lend a touch of luxury to any outfit.

Design by Elena Malo   Photograph by Tony Lattari

"The fragrance always stays in the hand that gives the rose."

—George William Curtis

TRIANGLE SHAWL
Easy ■ ■ ▢ ▢

SIZE
finished measurements
57×37"

SHOP
yarn
Boa from Bernat
(Art. 164081)
100% polyester; 1¾ oz. (50 g); 71 yds. (65 m); bulky weight
• 9 balls #81926 Sable

6 SUPER BULKY

hook & extra
• Size K/10½ (6.5 mm) crochet hook OR SIZE NEEDED TO OBTAIN GAUGE
• Blunt-end yarn needle

PREP
gauge
9 sts and 8 rows = 4" (10 cm) in hdc. TAKE TIME TO CHECK YOUR GAUGE.

CROCHET
Ch 122 loosely.
Row 1 (RS): Hdc in 3rd ch from hook and in each ch across—120 sts. Do not make turning ch; turn.
Row 2: Sk first st, hdc in each st to last st; do not work last st. Do not ch; turn.
Rep Row 2 for 47 more times—24 sts. Fasten off.

Cluster-Stitch Edging
Wth RS facing, join yarn with a sl st in any corner.
Rnd 1: ★Ch 4, in same st as joining, work as foll: [yo hook 4 times, insert hook into st (or row) and draw up a lp, (yo and draw through 2 lps on hook) 4 times] 4 times, yo and draw through all 5 lps on hook—cluster st made; sk next 2 sts (or rows), sc in next st (or row) to join; rep from ★ around, making sure to work 1 cluster st in each corner, join rnd with a sl st in first ch of beg ch-4; fasten off.
Weave in ends.

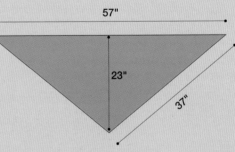

57"

23"

37"

pink and so *Pretty*

A combo of bias and mesh stitches transforms this shell into a top that's too pretty to hide under a jacket. It can go casual, over jeans, or dressy with a long skirt.

Design by Lily Chin   Photograph by Kathryn Gamble

PINK SHELL
experienced ■■ ■■ ■■ ■■

SIZES
S (M, L, 1X, 2X)
Instructions are written for the smallest size with changes for larger sizes given in parentheses. When only one number is given, it applies to all sizes. *Note:* For ease in working, circle all numbers pertaining to the size you're making.

finished measurements
Bust = 36 (39, 42, 45, 48)"
Length = 20¼ (21, 21½, 22, 22½)"

SHOP
yarn
Elite Cotton from Lily
100% cotton; 3½ oz. (100 g); 184 yds. (168 m); worsted weight

4 MEDIUM

• 6 (7, 8, 9, 10) balls #05415 Rose

hook & extras
• Size H/8 (5 mm) crochet hook OR SIZE NEEDED TO OBTAIN GAUGE
• Stitch markers
• Blunt-end yarn needle

PREP
gauge
16 hdc and 10 hdc rows = 4" (10 cm) in Body pat. 9 Mesh blocks and 7 rows = 4" (10 cm) in Mesh pat. TAKE TIME TO CHECK YOUR GAUGE.

stitch abbreviations
Af-lp (around the front lp) = Work the hdc around the horizontal strand that lies below the front lp of the hdc. Work the hdc in the front of the work.

Hdc2tog = (Yo and draw up a lp in next ch or st) twice, yo and draw through 5 lps on hook.

special stitch
Mesh st = (Dc, ch 1) across. On subsequent rows, *dc in dc, ch 1; rep from * across.

CROCHET
BODY
Note: Body is worked from side to side on the bias. Yoke is then picked up from side edge of body and worked upwards. Ch-1 at beg of row does NOT count as hdc. Hdc is always worked under the top 2 lps of the stitch unless specifically noted otherwise.

Loosely ch 61.
Row 1 (RS): Hdc in 2nd ch from hook, hdc2tog over next 2 ch—dec made; hdc in next 48 ch; 2 hdc in next ch—inc made—52 hdc. Place contrasting stitch marker to separate Body from trim. (Ch 1, dc in next ch) 4 times for mesh trim; turn.
Row 2: Ch 4—counts as dc and ch 1; (dc in next dc, ch 1) 3 times; ch 1, dc in same dc as last dc worked, ch 1—Mesh inc made; carry marker. Work 2 hdc in next hdc, work Af-lp in next 48 hdc; (yo and draw up lp, work Af-lp in next hdc) twice, yo and draw through all 5 lps on hook—Af-lp dec made;

hdc in last hdc—52 hdc for Body and 5 Mesh sts for trim; turn.
Row 3: Ch 1, hdc in first hdc, hdc2tog through back lps of next 2 hdc, hdc through back lp of next 48 hdc, 2 hdc in last hdc; move marker. Sk next ch of trim, in next dc work (ch 1, dc) twice; (ch 1, dc in next dc) 3 times, ch 1, dc in 3rd ch of ch-4 turning ch—52 hdc for Body and 6 Mesh sts for trim; turn.
Row 4: Ch 4—counts as dc and ch 1; (dc in next dc, ch 1) 5 times, work Mesh inc; move marker, 2 hdc in next hdc, work Af-lp in next 48 hdc, work Af-lp dec in next 2 hdc; hdc in last hdc—52 hdc for Body and 7 Mesh sts for trim; turn.
Row 5: Ch 1, hdc in first hdc, hdc2tog through back lps of next 2 hdc, hdc through back lps of next 48 hdc, 2 hdc in last hdc; carry marker, sk next ch of trim, (ch 1, dc) twice in next dc; (ch 1, dc in next dc) 5 times, ch 1, dc in 3rd ch of ch-4 turning ch—52 hdc for Body and 8 Mesh sts for trim; turn.
Row 6: Ch 4—counts as dc and ch 1; (dc in next dc, ch 1) 7 times; work Mesh inc; carry marker, 2 hdc in next hdc, work Af-lp in next 48 hdc, work Af-lp dec in next 2 hdc; hdc in last hdc—52 hdc for Body and 9 Mesh sts for trim; turn.
Row 7: Ch 1, hdc in first hdc, hdc2tog through back lps of next 2 hdc, hdc through back lps of next 48 hdc, 2 hdc in last hdc; carry marker. (Ch 1, dc in next dc) 4 times, sk last 5 meshes—52 hdc for Body and 4 Mesh sts for trim.

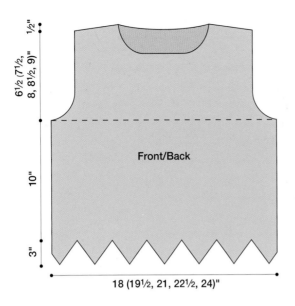

1/2"

6½ (7½,
8, 8½, 9)"

10"

3"

Front/Back

18 (19½, 21, 22½, 24)"

Rep Rows 2–7 for pat.

Work in pat until there are 72 (78, 84, 90, 96) rows total—12 (13, 14, 15, 16) trim triangles. Sew last row to beg foundation ch to form a tube, having bias seam beg at underarm.

Back Armholes

Row 1: Fold piece in half. With RS facing and working along the straight edge, sk and mark ½ (1, 1½, 1¾, 2¼)" from each fold. Join yarn with sl st, ch 3—counts as dc; (ch 1, dc) evenly across 38 (39, 40, 42, 43) times, ending with 1 dc at marked st—38 (39, 40, 42, 43) Mesh blocks across center 17 (17½, 18, 19, 19½)" of straight edge of Body; turn.

Shape Armholes

Row 2: Ch 3, dc in next dc—counts as beg dc dec; ★ch 1, sk next ch, dc in next dc; rep from ★ until 3 sts from end, ch 1, dec over next 2 dc—dc dec at end of row worked—36 (37, 38, 40, 41) Mesh blocks.
Row 3: Rep Row 2—34 (35, 36, 38, 39) Mesh blocks.
Row 4: Rep Row 2—32 (33, 34, 36, 37) Mesh blocks.
Work even in Mesh st until armhole measures approx 6¾ (7½, 8, 8½, 9)"; turn.

Shape Shoulders

Ch 1, sc in first dc, ch 1, sk next dc, sc in next dc, ch 1, (hdc in next dc, ch 1) twice; (dc in next dc, ch 1) 2 (2, 2, 3, 3) times; (tr in next dc, ch 1) twice, dc in next dc, ch 1, hdc in

next dc, ch 1, (sc in next dc, ch 1) 13 (14, 15, 15, 16) times, hdc in next dc, ch 1, dc in next dc, ch 1, (tr in next dc, ch 1) twice; (dc in next dc, ch 1) 2 (2, 2, 3, 3) times; (hdc in next dc, ch 1) twice, sc in next dc, ch 1, sc in next dc. Fasten off.

Front Armholes

Work as for back armholes until armholes measure approx 3¾ (4½, 5, 5½, 6)".

Shape Neck

Note: Neck and shoulders are worked at the same time with separate balls of yarn in the foll rows.
Work 10 (10, 10, 11, 11) Mesh blocks, dc next 2 dc tog; sk center 9 (10, 11, 11, 12) Mesh blocks; join separate ball of yarn to next dc, ch 2, sk next ch, dc in next dc for dec, work 10 (10, 10, 11, 11) Mesh blocks to end.
Next 3 rows: Work in mesh st and dec 2 sts from each neck edge in same manner as before—7 (7, 7, 8, 8) Mesh blocks at each shoulder.

Shape Shoulders

From armhole edge of first shoulder, ch 1 and turn, sc in first dc, ch 1, sc in next dc, ch 1, (hdc in next dc, ch 1) twice; (dc in next dc, ch 1) 2 (2, 2, 3, 3) times; tr in next dc, ch 1, tr in next dc. Fasten off.
From neck edge of 2nd shoulder, ch 5—counts as tr and ch 1; sk first dc and ch, tr in next dc, ch 1, (dc in next dc, ch 1) 2 (2, 2, 3, 3) times; (hdc in next dc, ch 1) twice, sk ch, sc in next dc, ch 1, sc in next dc. Fasten off.

FINISHING

Block Shell. Sew shoulder seams.
With RS facing, sc evenly around neck and armhole edges. Sc evenly around bottom, working an extra sc at points and dec at valleys of V-points.

A modified granny, faux cable pattern, and picot-style edging work their charms on this jacket standard—and add a feminine touch over even the sportiest Tee-and-jeans combo.

Design by Ann E. Smith
Photograph by Akin Girav

hooded Coat

> *"Romance is the glamour which turns the dust of everyday life into a golden haze."*
>
> —Amanda Cross

CAR COAT
Easy ▓▓ ▓▓ ☐ ☐

SIZES
S (M, L, 1X)
Instructions are written for the smallest size with changes for larger sizes given in parentheses. When only one number is given, it applies to all sizes. *Note:* For ease in working, circle all numbers pertaining to the size you're making.

finished measurements
Bust = 42 (47, 51½, 56½)"
Length = 26¾ (28, 28, 29¼)"

SHOP
yarn
Color Waves from Lion Brand (Art. 940)
73% acrylic, 17% polyester; 3 oz. (85 g); 125 yds. (118 m); bulky weight

• 8 (10, 11, 12) skeins #307 Caribbean

hook & extra
• Size K/10½ (6.5 mm) crochet hook OR SIZE NEEDED TO OBTAIN GAUGE
• Blunt-end yarn needle

PREP
gauge
10 sts and 6 rows = 4" (10 cm) in Faux Cable pat. 1 motif = 7" square. TAKE TIME TO CHECK YOUR GAUGE.

stitch abbreviations
Dc2tog = (Yo and draw up a lp in next st, yo and draw through 2 lps on hook) twice, yo and draw through all 3 lps on hook.
Sc2tog = Draw up a lp in each of next 2 sts, yo and draw through all 3 lps on hook.

CROCHET
PATTERN STITCH
Faux Cable Pattern
(multiple of 3 sts + 2)
Row 1 (RS): Ch 3—counts as dc; ★sk next sc, dc in next 2 sc, dc in skipped sc; rep from ★ across, ending with dc in last sc; turn.
Row 2: Ch 1, sc in each dc across; turn.
Rep Rows 1–2 for Faux Cable pat.

COAT
BACK
Motif (make 8)
Ch 8; join with sl st in first ch to form ring.
Rnd 1: Ch 1, work 12 sc in ring; join with sl st to first sc.
Rnd 2: Ch 5—counts as dc and ch 2; (in next sc work dc, ch 2) 11 times; join with sl st in 3rd ch of beg ch-5.
Rnd 3: Ch 3—counts as dc; ★3 dc in ch-2 sp, dc in next dc; rep from ★ around, ending 3 dc in last ch-2 sp—48 sts; join with sl st in 3rd ch of beg ch-3.
Rnd 4: Ch 1, 3 sc in same st as join; (sc in next 11 sts, 3 sc in next st) 3 times; sc in last 11 sc; join with sl st in first sc.
Rnd 5: Ch 1, sc in same st as join; in next sc work dc, ch 2, and dc for corner; ★sc in 13 sc; in next sc work dc, ch 2, and dc; rep from ★ around, ending with sc in last 12 sc; join with sl st to first sc; join and fasten off. With RS tog, sl st 4 motifs tog in a row. With RS facing, join yarn with sl st in corner ch-2 sp, ch 1, sc in same sp. ★Sc in next 15 sts, sc in next 2 ch-2 sps; rep from ★ across, end with sc in each of next 15 sts, sc in last ch-2 sp—68 sts; turn.
Next row: Ch 1, sc in each sc across AND AT THE SAME TIME dec 18 (12, 6, 0) sts evenly spaced across row—50 (56, 62, 68) sts; turn.
Begin Faux Cable pat and work even to approx 18¾ (20, 18¾, 20)" from beg, ending with a WS row.

Shape Armhole
Sl st in first 3 sc, in next sc work sl st, and ch 3—counts as dc; work in pat across to last 4 sts, dc in next sc, leave last 3 sc unworked; turn.
Work even on 44 (50, 56, 62) sts to approx 26¾ (28, 28, 29¼)" from beg, ending with a WS row; fasten off.

RIGHT FRONT
Sl st 2 motifs tog.
With RS facing, join yarn with sl st in corner ch-2 sp, ch 1, sc in same sp.
Sc in each of next 15 sts, sc in next 2 ch-2 sps, sc in each of next 15 sts, sc in last ch-2 sp—34 sts; turn.

Next row: Ch 1, sc in each sc across AND AT THE SAME TIME dec 11 (8, 5, 2) sts evenly spaced across row—23 (26, 29, 32) sts; turn. Begin Faux Cable pat and work even to approx 18¾ (20, 18¾, 20)" from beg, ending with a WS row.

Shape Armhole

Work in pat across to last 4 sc, dc in next sc, sk last 3 sc; turn. Work even on 20 (23, 26, 29) sts to 3 rows less than Back, ending with a RS row.

Shape Neck

Sc across and sk last 7 sts at neck edge— 13 (16, 19, 22) sts; turn.
Next row: Ch 3—counts as dc; dc2tog, work in pat across—12 (15, 18, 21) sts.
Next row: Sc across, ending with sc2tog— 11 (14, 17, 20) sts; fasten off.

LEFT FRONT

Work as for Right Front until piece measures approx 18¾ (20, 18¾, 20)" from beg, ending with a WS row.

Shape Armhole

Sl st in first 3 sc; in next sc work sl st and ch 3—counts as dc; work in pat across. Work even on 20 (23, 26, 29) sts to to 3 rows less than Back, ending with a RS row.

Shape Neck

Sl st in first 7 sts, in next st work sl st, ch 1, and sc, sc to end of row.
Next row: Work in pat across, end with dc2tog, dc in last dc.
Next row: Sc2tog, sc to end of row—11 (14, 17, 20) sts; fasten off.

Shape Hood Front

Beg at the front edge, ch 66. Sc in 2nd ch from hook and in each ch across—65 sts; turn. Ch 1, sc in each sc across; turn. Work Faux Cable pat until piece measures approx 7" from beg, ending with a RS row; fasten off.

Shape Hood Back

With WS facing, sk first 21 sts, join yarn with sl st in next st, ch 1, sc in same st and in next 22 sts; turn, leaving rem sts unworked. Work

even on the 23 sts until back measures same as skipped side sts; fasten off.
Sew back to skipped side sts. With RS facing, sc evenly around neck edge, leaving front sts free; fasten off. Set piece aside.

SLEEVE (make 2)

Beg at lower edge, ch 27. Sc in 2nd ch from hook and in each ch across—26 sts; turn. Ch 1, sc in each sc across; turn.
Work 2 Faux Cable pat rows.
Incorporating new sts into pat as they accumulate, inc 1 st each edge every other row 7 (7, 10, 10) times.
Work even on 40 (40, 46, 46) sts to approx 19¾" from beg, ending with a WS row; fasten off.

FINISHING

Join shoulder seams. With RS tog, sl st hood around neck of Coat.
Set in Sleeves, joining unworked sts to sides of Sleeves for square armholes. Join underarm and side seams.

Body Edging

Rnd 1: With RS facing, join yarn in a right ch-2 sp of one motif; ch 1, sc in same sp. Work 15 sc along each motif and 1 sc in each ch-2 sp. In corner motif, work 1 sc in first ch-2 sp, 15 sc along edge, and 3 sc in corner ch-2 sp. In same motif, work 15 sc along edge and 1 sc in ch-2 sp.
Work 40 (43, 43, 46) sc evenly spaced along front edge to Hood, 67 sc around Hood, and 40 (43, 43, 46) sc evenly spaced to first ch-2 sp of motif.
Sc as est along motifs, working 3 sc in corner. Join with sl st in first sc.
Rnds 2–3: Ch 1, sc in same sc as joining and in each sc around, working 3 sc in each corner; join.
Rnd 4: Sl st in next sc, in next sc work sl st, ch 3, and sl st—picot made; *sl st in next 2 sc, picot in next sc; rep from * around; fasten off.

Sleeve Edging

With RS facing, join yarn with sl st in first foundation ch at lower edge of Sleeve.
Sl st in same ch as join, work picot in next ch; *sl st in next 2 ch, picot in next ch; rep from * around; fasten off.

TIE (make 2)

Try on Coat to determine location of Ties. Place markers behind a picot on each edge for Tie placements. With RS facing, join yarn behind picot with a sl st, (ch 50, sl st in same sp as joining) twice; fasten off. Tie an overhand knot at end of each lp.

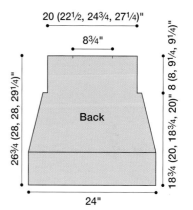

20 (22½, 24¾, 27¼)"

8¾"

26¾ (28, 28, 29¼)"

18¾ (20, 18¾, 20)" 8 (8, 9¼, 9¼)"

Back

24"

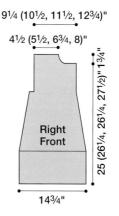

9¼ (10½, 11½, 12¾)"

4½ (5½, 6¾, 8)"

25 (26¼, 26¼, 27½)" 13¾"

Right Front

14¾"

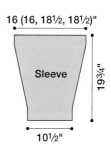

16 (16, 18½, 18½)"

Sleeve

19¾"

10½"

lilac and Lace

This openwork find is sublime over a filmy white blouse. Pair it with jeans or a ruffled skirt—the look is fabulous either way!

Design by Valerie Kurita   Photograph by Tony Lattari

CROPPED VEST
intermediate

SIZES
S (M, L)
Instructions are written for the smallest size with changes for larger sizes given in parentheses. When only one number is given, it applies to all sizes. *Note:* For ease in working, circle all numbers pertaining to the size you're making.

finished measurements
Note: This is a close-fitting garment, and the fronts of the vest do not meet at the center. The bow can be tied loosely to give additional width or tied tightly as shown in the photo.
Garment bust = 30 (34, 38)"
Fits actual bust = 32 (36, 40)"
Length = 17"

SHOP
yarn
Lacette from Patons (Art. 243030)
39% nylon, 36% acrylic, 25% mohair; 1¾ oz. (50 g); 235 yds. (215 m); baby weight
• 2 (3, 4) balls #30422 Lilac

hook & extras
• Size E/4 (3.5 mm) OR SIZE NEEDED TO OBTAIN GAUGE
• 1 yard of 2½"-wide cream silk ribbon
• Blunt-end yarn needle

PREP
gauge
10 (dc and ch-1) Mesh pat and 10 rows = 4" (10 cm). Rnd 1 of First Star Motif = 1" (2.5 cm) in diameter. TAKE TIME TO CHECK YOUR GAUGE.

Note: Fronts and Back are made the same for all sizes. Sizing is accomplished by working additional rows of sc along each side edge.

stitch abbreviation
Sc2tog = Draw up a lp in each of next 2 sts, yo and draw through all lps on hook.

CROCHET
BACK
Ch 82.
Row 1 (RS): Dc in 6th ch from hook—counts as 1 ch-1 mesh; ch 1, sk next ch, *dc in next ch, ch 1, sk next ch; rep from * across; dc in last ch—39 ch-1 mesh. Ch 3—counts as first dc of next row; turn.
Row 2: Dc in next ch-1 sp, *ch 1, dc in next ch-1 sp; rep from * across, end dc in 3rd ch of turning-ch 6—38 ch-1 mesh. Ch 4—counts as first dc and ch-1 of next row; turn.
Row 3: Dc in next ch-1 sp, *ch 1, dc in next ch-1 sp; rep from * across, end ch 1, dc in top of turning—39 ch-1 mesh. Ch 3, turn.
Rep Rows 2–3 for Mesh pat until piece measures 9" from beg, ending with a WS row.

Shape Armholes
Sl st in each st across first 3 sps, sl st in next dc, ch 4, work in Mesh pat as est across to last 3 sps, leave rem 3 sps unworked, ending last dc in dc—33 ch-1 mesh. Work even in pat on rem sts until armhole measures 8".

Edging
Rnd 1: With RS facing, work 1 rnd sc around entire Back, working 2 sc in each ch-1 sp along top and bottom edges, in each row along sides, and 5 sc in each corner sp. Join with sl st to first sc of rnd.
Rnd 2: Ch 1, sc in each sc around; join with sl st to first sc. Fasten off.

Sizes M and L Only:
With RS facing, join yarn at right side in lower corner and work back and forth in rows of sc along side edge only for 1 (2)", ending with a RS row. Do not work along armhole. Fasten off. Rep on rem side edge.

LEFT FRONT
First Star Motif
Ch 4, join with sl to form ring.
Rnd 1: Ch 4—counts as dc and ch 1; *dc in ring, ch 1; rep from * 6 more times, join last ch-1 with sl st to 3rd ch of starting ch-4—8 ch-1 sps.
Rnd 2: Sl st in next ch, ch 1, sc in same sp, ch 3, *sc in next sp, ch 3; rep from * 6 more times, join last ch-3 with sl st to first sc—8 ch-3 lps.
Rnd 3: Sl st in next ch, ch 1, sc in same lp, ch 9, *sc in next ch-3 lp, ch 9; rep from * 6 more times, join last ch-9 with sl st in first sc—8 ch-9 lps. Fasten off.

Second Star Motif

Work as for Rnds 1–2 of First Star Motif.

Rnd 3 (Joining rnd): Sl st in next ch, ch 1, sc in same lp, ch 4, pick up First Motif and hold WS tog with Second Motif, insert hook under 2 top lps of 5th ch of a ch-9 lp on First Motif and complete a sl st—joining made; ch 4, sc in next ch-3 lp on Second Motif, ch 4, work joining in next ch-9 lp on First Motif as before, ch 4, sc in next ch-3 lp on Second Motif, complete rem of rnd as for Rnd 3 of First Motif—2 joined ch-9 lps and 6 free ch-9 lps. Fasten off. Referring to Diagram 1, *page 30,* work and join 5 additional Star Motifs as shown, joining points as indicated.

First Filler Motif (A)

Rnd 1: Work as for Rnd 1 of First Star Motif.

Rnd 2: Sl st in next ch-1 sp, ch 1, sc in same sp, ch 1, pick up joined Star Motif piece and locate opening A as indicated on Diagram 2, *page 30;* hold WS tog with Filler Motif, work a sl st into any red dot indicated around opening A to join the 2 pieces, ch 1, ★sc in next sp on Filler Motif, ch 1, join Filler Motif to next red dot around opening A, ch 1; rep from ★ 6 more times, join with sl st to first sc. Fasten off.

Second Filler Motif (B)

Rnd 1: Work as for Rnd 1 of First Filler Motif.

Rnd 2: Sl st in next ch-1 sp, ch 1, sc in same sp, ch 3, sc in next sp, ch 1, now join as before in 7 red dots, as shown in Diagram 2, around opening B, leaving first ch-3 lp unjoined.

Third Filler Motif (C)

Rnd 1: Work as for Rnd 1 of First Filler Motif.

Rnd 2: Sl st in next ch-1 sp, ch 1, sc in same sp, (ch 3, sc in next sp) 3 times, ch 1, now join as before in 5 red dots, as shown in Diagram 2, around opening C, leaving first 3 ch-3 lps and adjacent points of 2 Star Motifs around opening C unjoined as shown.

Edging

Rnd 1: With RS facing and referring to Diagram 3, *page 30,* join yarn in spot indicated, ch 1, sc in same spot, ch 11 for

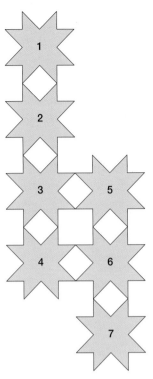

Left Front
Diagram 1 – Star Motifs

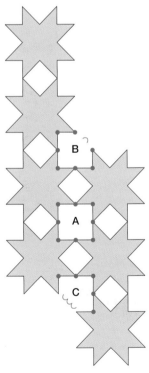

Left Front
Diagram 2 – Filler Motifs

Key

- • join Filler Motif with slst here
- ⌒ 1 unjoined ch-3 1p
- ⌒⌒⌒ 3 unjoined ch-31 ps

corner, sc in center ch of next ch-9 lp of same Star Motif, ch 3, sc in center ch of next ch-9 lp of same Star Motif, ch 11 for next corner and cont to foll Diagram 3 around entire joined piece, working either sc or tr in spot indicated, with number of ch bet sts as specified; join with sl st to first sc.

Rnd 2: Ch 1, sc in same sc, work sc in each sc and tr around and in each ch-sp work same number of sc as there were ch-sts on Rnd 1; join with sl st to first sc. Fasten off.

Sizes M and L Only:
With RS facing, join yarn on side edge in center st of lower corner and work back and forth in sc along side edge only for 1 (2)". Do not work along armhole. Fasten off.

RIGHT FRONT
Work as for Left Front, reversing position of Star Motifs. (Reverse diagram.)

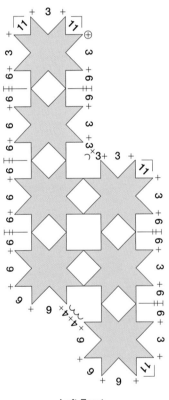

Left Front
Diagram 3 – Edging

Key
⊕ join here
Numbers number of chs bet sts
+ sc
⊹ sc in ch-9 1p of Star Motif
⌒ sc in ch-3 1p of Filler Motif
‡ tr

FINISHING
Sc tog side and shoulder seams. Using needle, weave in all yarn ends on WS of work.

Scallop Border
Note: Rnd 1 establishes the base for working Rnds 2–3. A multiple of 6 sts (in this pat, a multiple of 6 ch-1 sps) is essential for pat to come out even.

Rnd 1: With RS facing, join yarn at lower right side seam, ch 3—counts as hdc and ch 1; sk next st, *hdc in next st, ch 1; rep from * around, work to have a multiple of 6 ch-1 sps all around by skipping fewer or more sts spread out over several reps as necessary, join with sl st in 2nd ch of starting ch-3.

Rnd 2: Sl st in next ch-1 sp, ch 1, sc in same sp, sc in next sp, *3 dc in next sp, dc in next hdc, 3 dc in next sp, sc in each of next 4 sps; rep from * around, end last rep with sc in last 2 sps, join with sl st to first sc.

Rnd 3: Reach back and sl st in last sc of previous rnd (1 lp on hook), ch 1, sc2tog over this and next sc, *(dc in next dc, ch 3, sl st in 3rd ch from hook to form picot) 6 times, dc in next dc, sk next sc**, sc2tog over next 2 sc, sk next sc; rep from * around, end last rep at **; join with sl st to first sc2tog st. Fasten off.

Armholes
With RS facing, join yarn at underarm seam, work Scallop Border around armholes. Fasten off. Referring to Diagram 1, *left top,* pull ends of silk ribbon from WS to RS through openings bet 2 side points of Star Motif #4 or as desired. Tie ends in a bow.

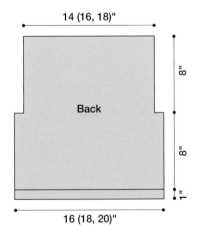

dreamy
Ruffles

Loops of soft yarn give this
trendy knee-length coat a
luxurious look all its own. The
neckline/front "ruffle" is worked
separately and sewn in place;
wrist ruffles are crocheted as
you work the sleeves.

Design by Gayle Bunn   Photograph by Akin Girav

> *"Dreams are true while they last, and do we not live in dreams?"*
>
> —Alfred Lord Tennyson

RUFFLED COAT
intermediate ■■■ ■■■ ■■■ ▢

SIZES
XS (S, M, L)
Instructions are written for the smallest size with changes for larger sizes given in parentheses. When only one number is given, it applies to all sizes. *Note:* For ease in working, circle all numbers pertaining to the size you're making.

finished measurements
Bust = 37 (39, 43, 47)"
Length = 38 (38½, 39, 39½)"

SHOP
yarn
Galaxy from Bernat (Art. 161053)
77% acrylic, 8% polyester, 7.5% mohair, 7.5% alpaca; 1¾ oz. (50 g); 60 yds. (55 m); bulky weight
• 18 (19, 21, 22) balls #53335 Comet

6 SUPER BULKY

hook & extras
• Size L/11 (8 mm) crochet hook OR SIZE NEEDED TO OBTAIN GAUGE
• One hook-and-eye closure
• Blunt-end yarn needle

PREP
gauge
12 sts and 9 rows = 5" (12 cm) in Body pat. TAKE TIME TO CHECK YOUR GAUGE.

stitch abbreviations
ML (make loop) = Work as though you are making a regular sc as follows: Insert hook into the next sc. Let the yarn in the LH wrap around the middle finger from the back and over the index finger, yo, and draw a lp through the sc; adjust yarn around the middle finger to make a 1½" long lp. Keeping the middle finger wrapped with the yarn, yo and draw yarn through the 2 lps on the hook.
Sc2tog = Draw up a lp in each of next 2 sts, yo and draw yarn through 3 lps on hook.

CROCHET
PATTERN STITCH
Body pattern
Row 1 (WS): Ch 1, sc in first sc; *ch 1, sk sc, sc in next sc; rep from * across; turn.
Row 2: Ch 1, sc in first sc, sc in next ch-1 sp; *ch 1, sk sc, sc in next ch-1 sp; rep from * across; end with sc in last sc; turn.
Row 3: Ch 1, sc in first sc; *ch 1, sk sc, sc in next ch-1 sp; rep from * to within 2 sc at end, ch 1, sk sc, sc in last sc; turn.
Rep Rows 2–3 for Body pat.

COAT
BACK
Ch 56 (58, 62, 68).
Row 1 (RS): Sc in 2nd ch from hook and in each ch across—55 (57, 61, 67) sts; turn.
Row 2: Ch 1; ML in each sc across; turn.
Row 3: Ch 1, sc in each st across; turn.
Rep last 2 rows until work measures approx 3½" from beg, ending with Row 3.
Work Body pat until approx 7" from beg, ending with a WS row.

Shape Side
Next row (RS): Ch 1, sc2tog over first sc and ch-1 sp; work pat across, ending with sc2tog over last ch-1 sp and last sc; turn.
Work 3 rows even in pat. Dec 1 st each end of NEXT and foll 8th row 3 more times—45 (47, 51, 57) sts. Cont in pat for approx 30", ending with a WS row.

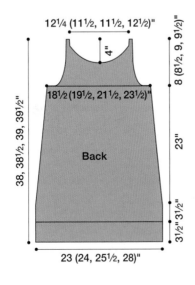

1½"
8 (8½, 9, 9½)"
23"
3½" 3½"
Left Front
7 (8, 8¾, 9½)"

12¼ (11½, 11½, 12½)"
4"
18½ (19½, 21½, 23½)"
8 (8½, 9, 9½)"
23"
3½"
38, 38½, 39, 39½"
Back
23 (24, 25½, 28)"

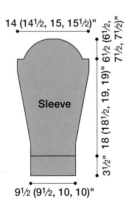

14 (14½, 15, 15½)"
6½ (6½, 7½, 7½)"
18 (18½, 19, 19)"
3½"
Sleeve
9½ (9½, 10, 10)"

Shape Armhole

Next row: Sl st in each of first 3 (4, 4, 6) sc; in next st work sl st, ch 1, and sc; work pat across, leaving last 3 (4, 4, 6) sts unworked—39 (39, 43, 45) sts; turn.

Dec 1 st each end of next 4 (4, 5, 5) rows—31 (31, 33, 35) sts. Work 2 (2, 3, 3) rows even.

Shape Shoulder and Back Neck

Right shoulder (RS): Ch 1, pat across 5 (5, 7, 9) sts; turn and leave rem sts unworked.

Dec 1 st at neck edge on next 4 rows—1 (1, 3, 5) st(s).

Work 1 (2, 1, 2) row(s) even in pat; fasten off. With RS facing, sk center 21 (21, 19, 17) sts for Back neck. Join yarn with sl st to next st, ch 1, sc in same st, work in pat to end of row—5 (5, 7, 9) sts; fasten off.

Work Left shoulder to correspond to Right shoulder.

LEFT FRONT

Ch 19 (21, 23, 25).

Row 1 (RS): Sc in 2nd ch from hook and in each across—18 (20, 22, 24) sts; turn.

Row 2: Ch 1, ML in each sc across; turn.

Row 3: Ch 1, sc in each st across; turn.

Rep last 2 rows until work measures approx 3½", ending with Row 3 and dec 1 st in center of last row—17 (19, 21, 23) sts.

Work in Body pat as for Back until work measures approx 7", ending with a WS row.

Shape Side

Dec 1 st at beg of NEXT and foll 8th row 3 more times—13 (15, 17, 19) sts.

Work even in pat until work measures 4 rows less than Back to beg of armhole shaping.

Dec 1 st at end of next row.

Work 3 rows even on 12 (14, 16, 18) sts.

Shape Armhole

Next row: Sl st in each of first 3 (4, 4, 6) sts; in next st work sl st, ch 1, and sc; work in pat across, ending with sc2tog over last 2 sts—8 (9, 11, 11) sts; turn. Dec 1 st at armhole on next 4 (4, 5, 5) rows, AND AT THE SAME TIME, dec 1 st at front edge on foll 4th row 3 more times—1 (2, 3, 3) st(s). Cont in pat until front piece measures same length as Back; fasten off.

RIGHT FRONT

Work to correspond to Left Front, reversing all shapings.

SLEEVE (make 2)

Ch 24 (24, 26, 26).

Row 1 (RS): Sc in 2nd ch from hook and in each ch across—23 (23, 25, 25) sts; turn.

Row 2: Ch 1, ML in each sc across; turn.

Row 3: Ch 1, sc in each st across; turn.

Rep last 2 rows until work measures approx 3½", ending with Row 3; place marker at end of last row.

Work in Body pat as for Back until Sleeve from marker measures approx 4", ending with a WS row.

Shape Side

Inc 1 st at each end of NEXT and foll 4th row until there are 33 (35, 37, 39) sts, working incs into pat.

Work even in pat until Sleeve from marker measures approx 18 (18½, 19, 19)", ending with a WS row.

Shape Sleeve Cap

Sl st in each of first 3 sts; in next st work sl st, ch 1, and sc; work in pat across, leaving last 3 sts unworked—27 (29, 31, 33) sts; turn.

Dec 1 st each end of every row until there are 5 (5, 5, 7) sts; fasten off.

FINISHING

Sew Fronts to Back at shoulders. Sew side seams, then Sleeve seams, reversing cuffs for turn-back. Set in Sleeves.

Edging

Ch 12.

Row 1 (RS): Sc in 2nd ch from hook, and in each ch across—11 sts; turn.

Row 2: Ch 1, ML in each sc across; turn.

Row 3: Ch 1, sc in each st across; turn.

Rep last 2 rows until strip measures length to fit up Right Front, around Back neck edge, and down Left Front, sewing in place as you go and ending with Row 3; fasten off.

Place a marker at each front edge 30" from bottom; sew hook-and-eye closure in place.

jacket Artistry

If exceptional styling is your passion, you'll fall head over heels for this glimmering, asymmetrical design.

Design by Anna Mishka   Photograph by Greg Scheidemann

ASYMMETRICAL JACKET
intermediate

SIZES
S (M, L, 1X)
Instructions are written for the smallest size with changes for larger sizes given in parentheses. When only one number is given, it applies to all sizes. *Note:* For ease in working, circle all numbers pertaining to the size you're making.

finished measurements
Bust (buttoned) = 36 (40, 44, 48)"

SHOP
yarn
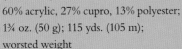
Lion Brand Glitterspun (Art. 990)
60% acrylic, 27% cupro, 13% polyester; 1¾ oz. (50 g); 115 yds. (105 m); worsted weight
• 8 (9, 9,10) balls #135 Bronze

hook and extras
• Size I/9 (5.5 mm) crochet hook OR SIZE NEEDED TO OBTAIN GAUGE
• Five ⅜"-diameter buttons
• Blunt-end yarn needle

PREP
gauge
5 tr2tog and 7½ rows = 4" (10 cm) in Lace pat.
18 sts and 18 rows = 4" (10 cm) in Seed st.
TAKE TIME TO CHECK YOUR GAUGE.

stitch abbreviation
Sc2tog = Draw up a lp in next 2 sts, yo and draw through all 3 lps on hook.

Note: Back is made in two separate pieces and then joined together.
Each ch-1 sp counts as one st, and each ch-2 sp counts as two sts.

CROCHET
PATTERN STITCH
Seed stitch
(multiple of 2 sts + 1; a rep of 2 rows)
Row 1 (WS): Ch 1, sc in first sc; *sc in next ch-1 sp, ch 1, sk next sc; rep from * across, ending sc in last ch-1 sp, sc in last sc; turn.
Row 2: Ch 1, sc in first sc; *ch 1, sk next sc, sc in next ch-1 sp; rep from * across, ending ch 1, sk next sc, sc in last sc; turn.
Rep Rows 1–2 for Seed st.

JACKET
RIGHT BACK
Beg at lower edge, ch 43 (43, 49, 49).

Begin Lace Pattern
Row 1 (RS): Sc in 2nd ch from hook and in each ch across—42 (42, 48, 48) sts; turn.
Row 2: Ch 5—counts as tr and ch-1; yo twice and draw up a lp in next st, (yo and draw through 2 lps on hook) twice, sk next 2 sc; yo twice and draw up a lp in next st, (yo and draw through 2 lps on hook) twice, yo and draw through all 3 lps on hook—beg

tr2tog made, ch 2. *Yo twice and draw up a lp in same sc as last st, (yo and draw through 2 lps on hook) twice, sk next 2 sc, yo twice and draw up a lp in next sc; (yo and draw through 2 lps on hook) twice, yo and draw through all 3 lps on hook—tr2tog made, ch 2; rep from * across, ending tr in last sc—13 (13, 15, 15) tr2tog; turn.
Row 3: Ch 1, sc in first tr; *2 sc in next ch-2 sp, sc in next st; rep from * across to last ch-5, sc in 5th and 4th ch of ch-5—42 (42, 48, 48) sc; turn.
Rep Rows 2–3 for Lace pat until piece measures 11" from beg, ending with Row 2.

Shape Armhole
Row 1 (RS): Sl st in first 6 sts, ch 1, sc in same st as last sl st, work in pat to end of row—37 (37, 43, 43) sc; turn.
Row 2: Work in pat across to last 2 sc, ch 1 (instead of ch 2), sk next sc, tr in last sc—11 (11, 13, 13) tr2tog; turn.
Row 3: Ch 1, work in pat across—35 (35, 41, 41) sc; turn.
Row 4: Work in pat to last 3 sc, ch 2, sk 2 sc, tr in last sc—10 (10, 12, 12) tr2tog; turn.
Row 5: Ch 1, work in pat to end of row—33 (33, 39, 39) sc; turn. Work even in pat until armhole measures approx 7½ (7½, 8½, 8½)", ending with a WS row; fasten off.

LEFT BACK
Ch 36 (42, 42, 52).
Foundation row (RS): Sc in 2nd ch from hook; *ch 1, sk next ch, sc in next ch; rep

from ★ across—35 (41, 41, 51) sts; turn.
Work Seed st until work from beg measures
7½", ending with a WS row.

Shape Armhole

Row 1 (RS): work in pat across, leaving last
5 sts unworked—30 (36, 36, 46) sts; turn.
Row 2: Ch 1, sc in first sc, sc2tog over next
2 sts, pat to end of row; turn.
Row 3: Ch 1, pat to end of row; turn.
Rep last 2 rows 4 (4, 4, 6) times more—
25 (31, 31, 39) sts; turn. Work even in pat
until armhole measures same length as Right
Back, ending with a WS row; fasten off.
Sew backs tog, leaving 3½" at lower edge of
Right Back free to form asymmetrical
bottom edge.

RIGHT FRONT

Ch 52 (58, 61, 67).
Row 1 (RS): Sc in 2nd ch from hook and
in each ch across—51 (57, 60, 66) sts; turn.
Rep Row 2 of Lace pat—16 (18, 19, 21)
tr2tog.
Row 3 of Lace pat. Rep last 2 rows of pat for
11", ending with a WS row.

Shape Armhole

Work in pat across, leaving last 5 sts
unworked—46 (52, 55, 61) sc.
Row 2: Ch 5—counts as tr and ch-1; sk
next sc, tr2tog over next 4 sts, work in pat to
end of row—14 (16, 17, 19) tr2tog; turn.
Row 3: Ch 1, work in pat to last ch-5, sk
5th ch, sc in 4th ch of ch-5—44 (50, 53, 59)
sc; turn.
Row 4: Ch 5—counts as tr and ch-1; sk
next 2 sc, tr2tog over next 4 sts, work in pat
to end of row—13 (15, 16, 18) tr2tog; turn.
Row 5: Ch 1, work in pat to end of row—
42 (48, 51, 57) sc; turn. Work even in pat
until armhole measures approx 4½ (4½, 5½,
5½)", ending with a RS row.

Shape Neck

Ch 5—counts as tr and ch-1; work 4 (5,
6, 7) tr2tog, ending ch 2, tr in last sc; leave
rem 27 (30, 30, 33) sc unworked; turn.
Rep Row 3—15 (18, 21, 24) sc; turn.
Work even in pat until armhole measures
same length as Back; end with a WS row.
Fasten off.

LEFT FRONT

Ch 24 (28, 32, 34).
Row 1 (RS): Sc in 2nd ch from hook; ★sk
next ch, sc in next ch; rep from ★ across—
23 (27, 31, 33) sts; turn.
Rep Rows 1–2 of Seed st until work from
beg measures 7½", ending with a WS row.

Shape Armhole

Sl st in first 6 sts, ch 1, sc in same st as last sl
st, work pat to end of row—18 (22, 26, 28)
sts; turn.
Row 2: Ch 1, sc in first sc, sc2tog over next
2 sts, work pat to end of row; turn.
Row 3: Ch 1, work pat to end of row; turn.
Rep last 2 rows 4 (4, 4, 6) more times—
13 (17, 21, 21) sts. Cont even in pat until
armhole measures same length as Right
Front. Fasten off.

SLEEVE (make 2)

Ch 34 (34, 40, 40).
Row 1 (RS): Sc in 2nd ch from hook, and
in each ch across—33 (33, 39, 39) sc; turn.
Rep Row 2 of Lace pat—10 (10, 12, 12)
tr2tog.
Rep Row 3 of Lace pat—33 (33, 39, 39) sc.
Rep last 2 rows of pat for 6", ending with
Row 2.
Next row (RS): Ch 1, sc in first tr; ★2 sc in
next ch-2 sp, sc in next st, 3 sc in next ch-2
sp, sc in next st; rep from ★ to last ch-5, 2 sc
in 5th ch, sc in 4th ch of ch-5—39 (39, 45,
45) sc; turn.
Next row: Ch 1, sc in first sc; ★sc in next sc,
ch 1, sk sc; rep from ★ across, end with sc in
next sc, ch 1, sk next sc, sc in last 2 sc; turn.
Next row: Ch 1, sc in first sc; ★ch 1, sk next
sc, sc in next sc; rep from ★ to last 2 sc; ch 1,
sk sc, sc in last sc, turn.
Rep last 2 rows of pat, working 2 sc in
first and last st on next and every foll 4th
row to 45 (45, 51, 51) sts, then every foll
6th row to 57 (57, 63, 63) sts, working incs
into pat.
Work even until Sleeve measures 17½"; end
with a WS row.

Shape Sleeve Cap

Sl st in first 4 sts, ch 1, sc in same st as last sl
st, work pat to last 3 sts and leave last 3 sts
unworked—51 (51, 57, 57) sts; turn.

Next row: Ch 1, sc in first sc, sc2tog over next 2 sts, work pat to last 3 sts, sc2tog over next 2 sts, sc in last st; turn.

Next row: Ch 1, pat to end of row; turn. Rep last 2 rows 3 (3, 5, 5) more times— 43 (43, 45, 45) sts.

Next row: Ch 1, sc in first sc, sc2tog over next 2 sts, work pat to last 3 sts, sc2tog over next 2 sts, sc in last st; turn.

Rep last row until 9 sts rem. Fasten off.

FINISHING

Sew shoulder seams; set in Sleeves, sew side and Sleeve seams.

With RS facing, join yarn to bottom right corner of Front, ch 1, 3 sc in same sp; sc evenly around, working 3 sc in each corner; join with sl st in first sc. Do not turn. Working left to right for reverse sc, ch 1, sc in each sc around. Fasten off.

Mark Left Front for placement of five buttons. First button is ½" from lower edge, last button is 4½" from shoulder seam, and rem three buttons are spaced evenly bet. Use holes of first round of sc as buttonholes. Sew on buttons.

Sleeve Edging

With RS facing, join yarn at underarm seam, ch 1, sc in same sp; sc evenly around; join with sl st in first sc.

Ch 1, work reverse sc around. Fasten off.

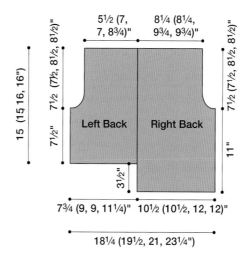

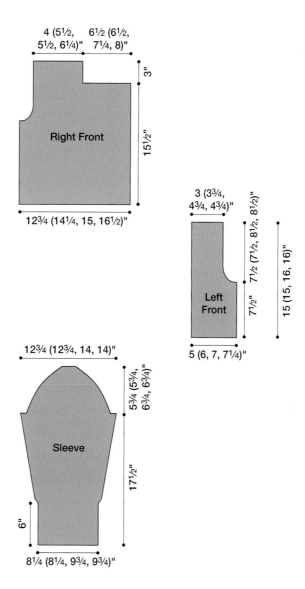

winter Enchantments

Soft white makes a fashion statement in and of itself, but this trio enhances the luxe look with plenty of high-relief post crochet stitches and bobbles galore.

Designs by Marianne Forrestal   Photographs by Tony Lattari

HAT, SCARF, AND MITTENS

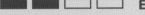 Easy

finished measurements
Hat: Circumference = 20"
Scarf: 10×72"
Mitten: Circumference = 9"
Length = 10½"

SHOP
yarn
Lion Cashmere Blend from Lion Brand (Art. 270)
72% merino wool, 14% cashmere, 14% nylon; 1½ oz. (40 g); 84 yds. (77 m); worsted weight
• 15 balls #098 Cream

hook & extra
• Size I/9 (5.5 mm) crochet hook OR SIZE NEEDED TO OBTAIN GAUGE
• Blunt-end yarn needle

PREP
gauge
12 hdc and 8 rows = 4" (10 cm). TAKE TIME TO CHECK YOUR GAUGE.

stitch abbreviations
BPdc = Yo, insert hook from back to front to back around post of st on row below, yo and draw up a lp, complete st same as regular dc.

FPdc = Yo, insert hook from front to back to front around post of st on row below, yo and draw up a lp, complete st same as regular dc.
FPtr = Yo twice, insert hook from front to back to front around post of st on row below, yo and draw up a lp, complete st same as regular treble crochet (tr).
Hdc-dec = (Yo, insert hook in next st, yo and pull up a lp) twice, yo and pull through all 5 lps.

special stitch
Bobble = (Yo, insert hook in st, yo and pull up a lp, yo and pull through 2 lps) 5 times, yo and pull through all 6 lps.

Note: Beg ch-2 counts as first hdc throughout.

CROCHET
HAT
Beg at brim, ch 61.
Row 1 (RS): Hdc in 3rd ch from hook, hdc in each ch across; turn—60 hdc.
Row 2: Ch 2, FPdc around next hdc, (BPdc around next hdc, FPdc around next hdc) 29 times, working last FPdc around turning-ch; turn.
Row 3: Ch 2, hdc in next 6 sts, (FPdc around next st, hdc in next 14 sts) 3 times, FPdc around next st, hdc in next 7 sts; turn.
Row 4: Ch 2, hdc in each st across; turn.
Row 5: Ch 2, hdc in next 4 sts, (FPtr around next FPdc on Row 3, hdc in next 3 sts, FPtr around same FPdc on Row 3, hdc in next 10 sts) 3 times, FPtr around next FPdc on

Row 3, hdc in next 3 sts, FPtr around same FPdc, hdc in last 5 sts; turn.
Row 6: Ch 2, hdc in each st across; turn.
Row 7: Ch 2, hdc in next 2 sts, (FPtr around next FPtr on Row 5, hdc in next 3 sts, Bobble in next st, hdc in next 3 sts, FPtr around next FPtr on Row 5, hdc in next 6 sts) 3 times, FPtr around next FPtr on Row 5, hdc in next 3 sts, Bobble in next st, hdc in next 3 sts, FPtr around next FPtr on Row 5, hdc in last 3 sts; turn.
Row 8: Ch 2, hdc in each st across; turn.
Row 9: Ch 2; FPtr around next FPtr on Row 7, hdc in next 3 sts, Bobble in next st, hdc in next 3 sts, Bobble in next st, hdc in next 3 sts, FPtr around next FPtr on Row 7, (hdc in next 2 sts, FPtr around next FPtr on Row 7, hdc in next 3 sts, Bobble in next st, hdc in next 3 sts, Bobble in next st, hdc in next 3 sts, FPtr around next FPtr on Row 7) 3 times; hdc in last st; turn.
Row 10: Ch 2, hdc in each st across; turn.
Row 11: Ch 2, hdc in next 6 sts, (Bobble in next st, hdc in next 6 sts, FPdc around both posts tog of next 2 FPtr on Row 9, hdc in next 6 sts) 3 times; Bobble in next st, hdc in last 7 sts; turn—57 sts.
Row 12: Ch 2, hdc in next 5 sts, (sk next st, hdc in next st, sk next st, hdc in next 11 sts) 3 times; sk next st, hdc in next st, sk next st, hdc in last 6 sts; turn—49 sts.
Row 13: Ch 2, hdc-dec, hdc in next 7 sts, (hdc-dec, FPdc around next FPdc on Row 11, hdc-dec, hdc in next 7 sts) 3 times; hdc-dec, hdc in last st; turn—41 sts.

Row 14: Ch 2, hdc in next st, (hdc-dec, hdc in next 3 sts) 7 times, hdc-dec, hdc in last 2 sts; turn—33 sts.

Row 15: Ch 2, hdc-dec, hdc in next 3 sts, (hdc-dec, FPdc around next FPdc on Row 13, hdc-dec, hdc in next 3 sts) 3 times, hdc-dec, hdc in last st; turn—25 sts.

Row 16: Ch 2, (hdc-dec, hdc in next st) 8 times; turn—17 sts.

Row 17: Ch 2, hdc in next st, hdc-dec, FPdc around next FPdc on Row 15, hdc in next st, hdc-dec, FPdc around next FPdc on Row 15, hdc-dec, hdc in next st, FPdc around next FPdc on Row 15, hdc-dec, hdc in last 2 sts; turn—13 sts.

Row 18: Ch 2, (hdc-dec, hdc in next st) 4 times; turn—9 sts.

Row 19: Ch 2, (sk next st, FPdc around next FPdc on Row 17) 3 times, sk next st, hdc in last st—5 sts; fasten off, leaving a 12" tail.

FINISHING

With WS facing, thread tail onto needle and weave through tops of sts on Row 19. Secure, cont sewing back seam to brim edge; cut yarn, leaving 8" tail; weave in end.

RUFFLED SCARF

Ch 18.

Row 1 (RS): Hdc in 3rd ch from hook and in each ch across; turn—17 hdc.

Row 2 and all WS rows: Ch 2, hdc in each st across; turn.

Row 3: Ch 2, hdc in next 7 sts, FPdc around next hdc, hdc in last 8 sts; turn.

Row 5: Ch 2, hdc in next 5 sts, FPtr around FPdc on Row 3, hdc in next 3 sts, FPtr around same FPdc on Row 3, hdc in last 6 sts; turn.

Row 7: Ch 2, hdc in next 3 sts, FPtr around next FPtr on Row 5, hdc in next 3 sts, Bobble in next st, hdc in next 3 sts, FPtr around next FPtr on Row 5, hdc in last 4 sts; turn.

Row 9: Ch 2, hdc in next st, FPtr around next FPtr on Row 7, (hdc in next 3 sts, Bobble in next st) twice, hdc in next 3 sts, FPtr around next FPtr on Row 7, hdc in last 2 sts; turn.

Row 11: Ch 2, FPtr around next FPtr on Row 9, hdc in next 6 sts, Bobble in next st, hdc in next 6 sts, FPtr around next FPtr on Row 9, hdc in last st; turn.

Row 13: Ch 2. FPdc around next FPtr on Row 11, hdc in next 13 sts, FPdc around next FPtr on Row 11, hdc in last st; turn.

Row 14: Ch 2, hdc in each st across; turn.

Rows 15–146: Rep Rows 3–14 for 11 more times; do not fasten off.

Border

Rnd 1 (RS): Sc in each hdc across, sc in side of first row, 2 sc in side of next row, (sc in side of next row, 2 sc in side of next row) 72 times, sc in each ch of starting ch, sc in side of first row, 2 sc in side of next row, (sc in side of next row, 2 sc in side of next row) 72 times; join with sl st to first sc—474 sc.

Rnd 2: Ch 4—counts as tr; 2 tr in same st, 2 tr in next st, (3 tr in next st, 2 tr in next st) around; join with sl st to top of beg ch-4.

Rnd 3: Tr in each tr around; join with sl st to top of beg ch-4; fasten off.

BOBBLE MITTENS

Right Mitten

Ch 21, join with sl st to first ch.

Rnd 1 (RS): Ch 2, hdc in each ch around; join with sl st to top of beg ch-2; turn—21 hdc.

Rnd 2 (WS): Ch 2, (FPdc around next st, BPdc around next st) 10 times; join with sl st to top of beg ch-2; turn.

Rnds 3–6: Ch 2, (BPdc around next st, FPdc around next st) 10 times; join with sl st to top of beg ch-2; turn.

Rnd 7: Ch 2, hdc in next st, 2 hdc in next st, (hdc in next 2 sts, 2 hdc in next st) 6 times; join with sl st to top of beg ch-2; turn—28 sts.

Rnds 8, 10, 12, and 14: Ch 2, hdc in each st around; join with sl st to top of beg ch-2; turn.

Rnd 9: Ch 2, hdc in next 7 sts, FPdc around next st, hdc in last 19 sts; join with sl st to top of beg ch-2; turn.

Rnd 11: Ch 2, hdc in next 5 sts; FPtr around FPdc on Rnd 9, hdc in next 3 sts, FPtr around same FPdc on Rnd 9, hdc in last 17 sts; join with sl st to top of beg ch-2; turn.

Rnd 13: Ch 2, hdc in next 3 sts, FPtr around next FPtr on Rnd 11, hdc in next 3 sts, Bobble in next st, hdc in next 3 sts, FPtr around next FPtr on Rnd 11, hdc in last 15 sts; join with sl st to top of beg ch-2; turn.

Rnd 15: Ch 2, hdc in next st, FPtr around next FPtr on Rnd 13; (hdc in next 3 sts, Bobble in next st) twice; hdc in next 3 sts, FPtr around next FPtr on Rnd 13, hdc in last 13 sts; join with sl st to top of beg ch-2; turn.

Rnd 16: Ch 2, hdc in next 7 sts, ch 4, sk next 4 sts, hdc in last 16 sts; join with sl st to top of beg ch-2; turn.

Rnd 17: Ch 2; FPtr around next FPtr on Rnd 15, hdc in next 6 sts, Bobble in next st, hdc in next 6 sts, FPtr around next FPtr on Rnd 15, hdc in next 4 chs, hdc in last 8 sts; join with sl st to top of beg ch-2; turn.

Rnds 18, 20, 22, and 24: Ch 2, hdc in each st around; join with sl st to top of beg ch-2; turn.

Rnd 19: Ch 2, FPdc around next FPtr on Rnd 17, hdc in next 13 sts, FPdc around next FPtr on Rnd 17, hdc in last 12 sts; join with sl st to top of beg ch-2; turn.

Rnd 21: Ch 2, hdc in next st, hdc-dec, (hdc in next 2 sts, hdc-dec) 6 times; join with sl st to top of beg ch-2; turn—21 sts.

Rnd 23: Ch 2; hdc-dec, (hdc, hdc-dec) 6 times; join with sl st to top of beg ch-2; turn—14 sts.

Rnd 25: Ch 2; (hdc-dec) 3 times, hdc, (hdc-dec) 3 times; join with sl st to top of beg ch-2—8 sts; fasten off, leaving a 6" tail for closing.

Thumb

With RS facing, join yarn with sl st to first skipped hdc of Rnd 16.

Rnd 1 (RS): Ch 2, hdc in next 3 sts, 2 hdc in side of row, hdc in each ch of ch-4 on Row 16, 2 hdc in side of row; join with sl st to top of beg ch-2; turn—12 hdc.

Rnd 2: Ch 2, hdc in each st around; join with sl st to top of beg ch-2; turn.

Rnds 3–4: Ch 2, hdc in each st around; join with sl st to top of beg ch-2; turn.

Rnd 5: Ch 2; (hdc-dec) twice, hdc, (hdc-dec) 3 times; join with sl st to top of beg ch-2—7 sts; fasten off, leaving a 6" tail for closing.

FINISHING

Turn Mitten inside out. Thread 6" tail onto yarn needle and weave through tops of sts on Rnd 5 of thumb. Pull tight and secure.
Rep on Rnd 25 of Mitten to close end.
Weave in ends. Turn RS out.

Left Mitten

Rep Rnds 1–8 of Right Mitten.

Rnd 9: Ch 2, hdc in next 18 sts, FPdc around next hdc, hdc in last 8 sts; join with sl st to top of beg ch-2; turn.

Rnds 10, 12, and 14: Ch 2, hdc in each st around; join with sl st to top of beg ch-2; turn.

Rnd 11: Ch 2, hdc in next 16 sts, FPtr around FPdc on Rnd 9, hdc in next 3 sts, FPtr around same FPdc on Rnd 9, hdc in last 6 sts; join with sl st to top of beg ch-2; turn.

Rnd 13: Ch 2, hdc in next 14 sts, FPtr around next FPtr on Rnd 11, hdc in next 3 sts, Bobble in next st, hdc in next 3 sts, FPtr around next FPtr on Rnd 11, hdc in last 4 sts; join with sl st to top of beg ch-2; turn.

Rnd 15: Ch 2, hdc in next 12 sts, FPtr around next FPtr on Rnd 13, (hdc in next 3 sts, Bobble in next st) twice, hdc in next 3 sts, FPtr around next FPtr on Rnd 13, hdc in last 2 sts; join with sl st to top of beg ch-2; turn.

Rnd 16: Hdc in next 15 sts, ch 4, sk next 4 sts, hdc in last 8 sts; join with sl st to top of beg ch-2; turn.

Rnd 17: Ch 2, hdc in next 7 sts, hdc in next 4 chs, FPtr around next FPtr on Rnd 15, hdc in next 6 sts, Bobble in next st, hdc in next 6 sts, FPtr around next FPtr on Rnd 15, hdc in last st; join with sl st to top of beg ch-2; turn.

Rnd 18: Ch 2, hdc in each st around; join with sl st to top of beg ch-2; turn.

Rnd 19: Ch 2, hdc in next 11 hdc, FPdc around next FPtr on Rnd 17, hdc in next 13 sts, FPdc around next FPtr on Rnd 17, hdc in last st; join with sl st to top of beg ch-2; turn.

Rep Rnds 20–25 of Right Mitten.
Work thumb and finish same as for Right Mitten.

shawl a-Shimmer

Little medallions of crochet turn dramatic when worked in yarns with sparkle and texture.

Design by Elena Malo   Photograph by Tony Lattari

PICOT SHAWL
Easy ■■ ■■ ▢ ▢

SIZE
One size fits most.

finished measurements
16×60"

SHOP
yarns
Brilliant from Patons
(Art. 246103—light shades;
Art. 246104—dark shades)
69% acrylic, 19% nylon, 12% polyester; 1¾ oz. (50 g); 166 yds. (152 m); DK weight
• 6 balls #03023 Gold Glow (A)
• 6 balls #04913 Marvelous Mocha (B)
• 3 balls #03008 Crystal Cream (C)

3 LIGHT

hook & extra
• Size H/8 (5 mm) crochet hook OR SIZE NEEDED TO OBTAIN GAUGE
• Blunt-end yarn needle

PREP
gauge
Large Motif = 4" (10 cm) across.
Small Motif = 2" (5 cm) across. TAKE TIME TO CHECK YOUR GAUGE.

special stitches
Picot = Ch 3, sl st in front lp of last dc.
Picot Cluster = (Ch 3, sl st in 3rd ch from hook) 3 times.

Note: For experienced crocheters, motifs can be joined tog as you work 4th rnd of Large Motifs, and 2nd rnd of Small and Half Small Motifs. Join them as you work picots and picot clusters. Work the first ch, then sl st into matching picot (on picot clusters, join only the center picot) of motif you are joining to, then complete picot for motif in progress. When finished, all motifs are joined tog using this technique. Half Small Motifs are joined last; picots are sl st to picot clusters of Large Motifs.

CROCHET
Beg at base, ch 47.

LARGE MOTIF #1 (make 30)
With C, ch 5; join with sl st to first ch to form ring.
Rnd 1: Work 12 sc in ring; join with B with sl st to first sc.
Rnd 2: With B, ch 3—counts as dc; dc in same st as last sl st, 2 dc in each sc around; join A with sl st to top of ch-3—24 dc.
Rnd 3: With A, ch 1, sc in same st as last sl st, ★ch 5, sk next 2 dc, sc in next dc; rep from ★ 6 more times, ch 5, sk next 2 dc; join with sl st to first sc.
Rnd 4: Ch 1, in each ch-5 lp around work: sc, hdc, 2 dc, cluster picot, sl st in front lp of last dc worked, 2 dc, hdc, and sc; join with sl st in first sc; fasten off.

LARGE MOTIF #2 (make 30)
Work as for Large Motif #1, beg with B for Rnd 1, C for Rnd 2, and A for Rnds 3–4.

SMALL MOTIF #3 (make 42)
With B, ch 8; join with sl st to first ch to form ring.
Rnd 1: Ch 1, 16 sc in ring; join with sl st to first sc.
Rnd 2: Ch 3—counts as dc; dc in same st as last sl st, 2 dc in next sc, make picot, ★2 dc in each of next 2 sc, make picot; rep from ★ around; join with sl st in top of ch 3— 8 picots; fasten off.

HALF SMALL MOTIF #4 (make 34)
With B, ch 2.
Row 1: Work 8 sc in 2nd ch from hook; turn.
Row 2: Ch 3—counts as dc; dc in first sc, make picot, ★2 dc in each of next 2 sc, make picot; rep from ★ twice more, 2 dc in last sc; fasten off.

FINISHING
Referring to the diagram, *opposite*, assemble Large Motifs in rows, 4 motifs wide by 15 motifs long, alternating #1 and #2. Sew in Small Motifs. Sew in Half Motifs around edge of Shawl.

Center Row

Picot Shawl
Assembly Diagram

crochet Basics

Here's all the information you'll need: stitch instructions, abbreviations, and skill level information to help you select an easy project or one that will stretch your abilities.

slip knot

1. Make a loop around hook; then hook another loop through it.
2. Tighten gently and slide the knot up to the hook.

chain stitch (ch)

1. Make a slip knot. Yarn over hook and draw the yarn through to form a new loop without tightening up the previous one.
2. Repeat to form as many chains as required. Do not count the slip knot as a chain stitch.

slip stitch (sl st)

This is the shortest crochet stitch and, unlike other stitches, is not used on its own to produce a fabric. It is used for joining, shaping, and, where necessary, carrying the yarn to another part of the fabric for the next stage.
1. Insert the hook into the work (second chain from hook), yarn over, and draw the yarn through both the work and the loop on the hook in one movement.
2. To join chains into a ring with a slip stitch, insert the hook into the first chain, yarn over, and draw through both the work and the yarn on the hook in one movement.

treble crochet (tr)

1. Yarn over the hook two times and insert the hook into the work (fifth chain from the hook on the starting chain).
2. Yarn over the hook and draw through the work only—four loops are on the hook.
3. Yarn over the hook and draw through the first two loops on the hook—three loops are on the hook.
4. Yarn over the hook and draw through the next two loops on the hook—two loops remain on the hook.
5. Yarn over the hook again and draw through remaining two loops on hook—one treble crochet made.

single crochet (sc)

1. Insert the hook into the work (second chain from hook on the starting chain), *yarn over the hook, and draw up a loop through the work only—two loops are on the hook.
2. Yarn over the hook again and draw the yarn through both loops on the hook—one single crochet made.
3. Insert the hook into the next stitch; repeat from * in step 1.

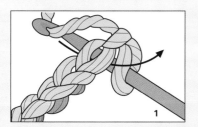  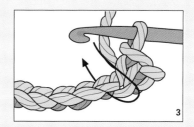

half double crochet (hdc)

1. Yarn over the hook and insert the hook into the work (third chain from the hook on the starting chain).
2. Yarn over the hook and draw up a loop through the work only—three loops on the hook.
3. Yarn over the hook again and draw through all three loops on the hook—one half double crochet made.
4. Yarn over the hook, insert the hook into the next stitch; repeat from step 2.

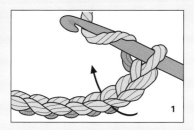 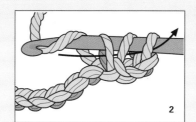 

double crochet (dc)

1. Yarn over the hook and insert the hook into the work (fourth chain from the hook on the starting chain).
2. Yarn over the hook and draw through the work only—three loops are on the hook.
3. Yarn over the hook and draw through the first two loops only—two loops are on the hook.
4. Yarn over the hook and draw through the last two loops on the hook—one double crochet made.
5. Yarn over the hook, insert the hook into the next stitch; repeat from step 2.

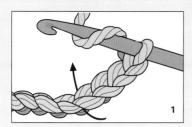  

reverse single crochet

This neat, narrow edging is perfect for finishing the edges of a crochet project. The important thing to remember is that you work this stitch from left to right instead of right to left—that's why it's called reverse single crochet. (The stitch is also referred to as a backward stitch or crab stitch.)

1. Starting on the left side of the crocheted piece, pull a slip knot through the end stitch. Chain one. *Draw up a loop in the next stitch to the right. Catch the yarn with the hook and pull it through the fabric and under but not through the loop already on the hook.

2. Bring the yarn over and around the top of the hook. Draw the yarn through both loops on the hook. Repeat from * in step 1.

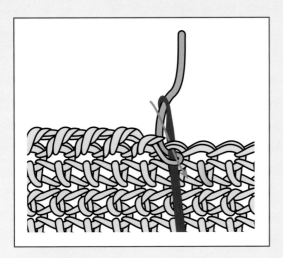

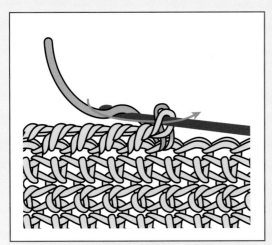

working in the front post

Follow the stitch instructions, inserting the hook around the post (the length of the stitch) in the row below (or as indicated) from front to back to front again.

working in the back post

Work as for a front-post stitch, except insert the hook from back to front to back again.

working in the back loops

• Working stitches in the back loops results in a ridge on the side that faces you.

• The pattern directions will indicate when to work in the back loops. (When directions are not specific, always work under the two top loops of the stitches.)

• Working in the back loops means you work in the back single strand of the stitch of the previous row. When working in rows, you must tilt your work to locate the strand; when working in rounds, this strand lies along the rim of the outside edge.

working in the front loops

The pattern may indicate you are to work in the front loops of the stitches, creating a ridge on the opposite side. In this case, work the stitches in the front strand of the stitch of the previous row.

skill levels defined

■□□□ BEGINNER: Projects for first-time crocheters are labeled "Beginner." These patterns use basic stitches, minimal shaping, and very simple finishing.

■■□□ EASY: Projects labeled "Easy" use basic stitches, repetitive stitch patterns, simple color changes, and simple shaping and finishing.

■■■□ INTERMEDIATE: Projects labeled "Intermediate" use a variety of techniques, such as lace or color patterns, with midlevel shaping and/or finishing.

■■■■ EXPERIENCED: Projects labeled "Experienced" use advanced techniques and stitches, with detailed shaping and refined finishing.

abbreviations

approx	approximately	hdc2tog	half double crochet 2 stitches together	[ ]	work instructions within brackets as many times as directed
beg	begin(ning)(s)	inc	increase(ing)		
bet	between	lp(s)	loop(s)		
BPdc	back post double crochet	MC	main color	( )	work instructions within parentheses as many times as directed
CC	contrasting color	pat	pattern		
ch	chain	rem	remain(ing)(s)		
ch-	refers to chain or space previously made	rep	repeat		
		rnd(s)	round(s)	*	repeat the instructions following the single asterisk as directed
ch-sp	chain-space	RS	right side		
cont	continue	sc	single crochet		
dc	double crochet	sc2tog	single-crochet 2 stitches together		
dc cl	double crochet cluster			**	repeat instructions between asterisks as many times as directed, or repeat from a set of instructions (sometimes you will see as many as three or four sets of asterisks; the same directions apply)
dc2tog	double-crochet 2 stitches together	sc3tog	single-crochet 3 stitches together		
		sk	skip		
dec	decrease(ing)	sl st	slip stitch		
end	ending	sp(s)	space(s)		
est	established	st(s)	stitch(es)		
foll	follow(ing)(s)	tog	together		
FPdc	front post double crochet	tr	treble crochet		
		tr cl	treble crochet cluster		
FPsc	front post single crochet	WS	wrong side	"	inch(es)
FPtr	front post treble crochet	yo	yarn over		
hdc	half double crochet				

Better Homes and Gardens®
Creative Collection®

Editorial Director John Riha

Editor in Chief Deborah Gore Ohrn

Executive Editor Karman Wittry Hotchkiss

Managing Editor Kathleen Armentrout

Contributing Editorial Manager Heidi Palkovic

Contributing Design Director Tracy DeVenney

Contributing Editor Laura Holtorf Collins
Contributing Designer Tracy DeVenney
Copy Chief Mary Heaton
Contributing Copy Editor Jennifer Horejsi
Proofreader Joleen Ross
Administrative Assistant Lori Eggers

Publishing Group President
Jack Griffin

President and CEO Stephen M. Lacy

Chairman of the Board William T. Kerr

In Memoriam
E. T. Meredith III (1933–2003)
